Native American
Historical Demography

BIBLIOGRAPHICAL SERIES

*The Newberry Library Center
for the History of the American Indian*

General Editors
Francis Jennings
Martin Zanger
Staff Editor
Joseph Narun

The Center is Supported by Grants from

The National Endowment for the Humanities
The Ford Foundation
The W. Clement and Jessie V. Stone Foundation
The Woods Charitable Fund, Inc.

Native American Historical Demography

A Critical Bibliography

HENRY F. DOBYNS

Published for the Newberry Library
Indiana University Press
BLOOMINGTON AND LONDON

Copyright © 1976 by Indiana University Press
All rights reserved
No part of this book may be reproduced or utilized in any form or by any means, electronic or mechanical, including photocopying and recording, or by any information storage and retrieval system, without permission in writing from the publisher. The Association of American University Presses' Resolution on Permissions constitutes the only exception to this prohibition.
Published in Canada by Fitzhenry & Whiteside Limited, Don Mills Ontario
Manufactured in the United States of America

Library of Congress Cataloging in Publication Data
Dobyns, Henry F
Native American historical demography.
(The Newberry Library Center for the History of the American Indian bibliographical series)
1. Indians—Population—Bibliography. 2. Indians of North America—Population—Bibliography.
I. Title. II. Series: Newberry Library, Chicago. Center for the History of the American Indian. The Newberry Library Center for the History of the American Indian bibliographical series.
Z1209.D58 [E59.P75] 016.97'0004'97 76-12371
ISBN 0-253-33974-0 1 2 3 4 5 80 79 78 77 76

The Editors to the Reader

A massive literature exists for the history and culture of American Indians, but the quality of that literature is very uneven. At its best it compares well with the finest scholarship and most interesting reading to be found anywhere. At its worst it may take the form of malicious fabrication. Sometimes, well-intentioned writers give false impressions of reality either because of their own limitations of mind or because they lack adequate information. The consequence is a kind of chaos through which advanced scholars as well as new students must warily pick their way. It is, after all, a history of hundreds, if not thousands, of human communities spread over an entire continent and enduring through millenia of pre-Columbian years as well as the five centuries that Europeans have documented since 1492. That is not a small amount of history.

Often, however, historians have been so concerned with the affairs of European colonies or the United States that they have almost omitted Indians from their own history. "Frontier history" and the "history of Indian–White relations" frequently focus upon the intentions and desires of Euramericans, treating Native Americans as though they were merely natural parts of the landscape, like forests, or mountains, or wild animals — obstacles to "progress" or "civilization." One of the major purposes of the Newberry Library's Center for the History of the American Indian is to modify that narrow conception; to put Indians properly back into the central role in their own history and into the history of the United States of America as well — as participants in, rather than obstacles to, the creation of American society and culture.

The series of bibliographies, of which this book is one part, is intended as a guide to reliable sources and studies in particular fields of the general literature. Some of these are devoted to culture areas; others treat selected individual tribes; and a third group will speak to significant contemporary and historical issues.

The present book is one of the most important in the series because it deals with the vital question of the capacity of Indian communities to grow and prosper before they were introduced to European technology. Traditionally, scholars have assumed that aboriginal Indian populations were very small, and that their smallness proved such inability to cope with the natural environment that the land remained "virgin" wilderness which a few scattered tribes "roamed through rather than inhabited." Assumptions of this sort have been used to argue that Indians had no moral or legal right of possession in the lands on which they lived. Dr. Dobyns points to sources and studies that evidence much larger pre-Columbian populations than have hitherto been suspected. No serious student of Native American society and history can afford to be unfamiliar with this literature.

This work is designed in a format, uniform throughout the entire series, to be useful to both beginning students and advanced scholars. It has two main parts: the essay (conveniently organized by subheadings) and an alphabetical list of all works cited. All citations in the essay are directly keyed, by means of bracketed numbers, to the more complete information in the list. In addition, the series incorporates several information-at-a-glance features. Preceding the list will be found two sets of recommended titles. One of these is a list of five items for the beginner; the second, a group of volumes that constitute a basic library collection in the field. Finally, asterisks within the alphabetical list denote works suitable for secondary school students. This apparatus has been built-in because the bibliographical essay, in a form familiar to scholars, will probably prove fairly hard going for beginners who may wish to put it aside until they have gained sufficient background from introductory materials. Such students should come back to the essay eventually, however, because it surveys a vast sweep of information about a great variety of persons, places, communities, and events.

There is variety also in the kinds of sources because these critical bibliographies support the study of ethnohistory. Unlike older, more narrow disciplines, ethnohistory embraces the entire culture of a people; it demands contributions from a wide range of source materials. Not the least of these in the history of American Indians are their own music, crafts, linguistics, and oral traditions. Whenever possible, the authors have included such sources as well as those associated with politics, economics, geography, and so on.

In the last analysis this work, like all other bibliographical devices, is a tool. Each author is an expert who knows the literature and advises what source is most helpful for which purpose, but students must use this help according to their individual purposes and capacities. Many ways suggest themselves. The decision is the reader's own.

Introduction

European explorers found North America populated by dark-skinned natives. Their present descendants are best termed "Native Americans" in our multi-ethnic society. Yet a high proportion of today's Native Americans actually are genetically mixed descendants of both Europeans and the aboriginal population of the Americas. While the dynamics of Native American historic population changes have been relatively little studied, they are neither mysterious nor exotic.

The Americas were densely populated at the time Europeans found their way to this New World. Recent estimates place the hemispheric population at 100,000,000 in about 1490. Perhaps two-fifths of that total inhabited North America, including the civilized states in Mexico (which contained some 30,000,000 people). Native Americans achieved those densities during prehistoric times because they inhabited a relatively disease-free paradise and domesticated high-yield cereals and tubers. Europeans destroyed that paradise—not intentionally, but simply because they carried Old World disease agents. Native Americans lacked immunities or resistance to Old World pathogens, and even lacked knowledge of nursing techniques for the care of the ill.

Smallpox became the single most lethal disease Europeans carried to the New World. This contagion repeatedly spread through Native American peoples, killing a high proportion of susceptible individuals not immunized by surviving a previous epidemic. Malaria and yellow fever strongly reinforced the decimating impact of smallpox, especially in low altitude coastal areas in the tropics. Plague, typhus, and influenza took a heavy toll among Native Americans living at all altitudes.

Colonial wars compounded the lethal impact of pathogens. European powers frequently battled against Native Americans resisting colonization, throwing into those frays armored men and warhorses, war-dogs and firearms, steel swords and sabers. Native Americans initially lacked all such elements of military superiority. Direct military confrontation between Europeans and Native Americans cost fewer lives among the latter, however, than did colonial wars which pitted tribe against tribe. Each European nation attempted to acquire a colonial empire in North America, and recruited tribal leaders to launch their tribesmen into battle against the tribal allies of competing colonial powers. England, France, Spain, the Netherlands, Sweden, and Russia all formed alliances with North American tribes.

Native Americans quickly succumbed to the lures of European technology. Firearms and ammunition, steel knives, axes, tomahawks, iron and copper pots, silver gorgets and other ornaments, and European woolen and cotton textiles rapidly displaced bows and arrows, stone blades and axes, ceramic pots and shell and other jewelry, and tanned animal skins and native cotton textiles. To pay for their imported manufactured goods, Native Americans necessarily exported goods in high demand in Europe. For most of the colonial period in most of North America, furs comprised the main export. The fur trade compounded the effects of introduced disease and colonial warfare. The drive for furs generated even more inter-tribal conflict, such as that mounted by the Five Nations against the Hurons in the mid-seventeenth century. Such wars of territorial conquest were not only themselves deadly, but they also fostered the spread of infection and disrupted traditional economic patterns.

Territorial warfare and increasing dependence upon the fur trade for supplies — even basic foodstuffs — exposed tribal peoples to famine. Acute food shortages weakened many populations, again heightening the impact of infectious diseases and increasing casualties sustained in battle. By the time these factors had achieved their full effect, a typical tribe would suffer serious food shortages one year in four.

Fur traders also introduced distilled alcoholic beverages to Native Americans. The physiological and cultural consequences proved disastrous for the New World aboriginal peoples. Intoxicated negotiators squandered tribal and individual land resources; embarked on senseless and counterproductive military adventures; and neglected horticultural food production tasks. Alcoholism apparently diminished male sexual potency, accelerating the rate of depopulation achieved directly by other factors.

Eventually, most Native Americans susceptible to Old

World disease agents simply perished. European nations reached the limits of their continental expansion or lost their North American footholds, decreasing colonial warfare. Public health measures discovered or invented in the Old World spread to North America — most notably vaccination against smallpox. Death rates fell among Native Americans. Many tribal peoples acquired Old World domestic animals. With cattle, swine, sheep, and goats, they developed a dependable source of food, especially the animal proteins so important for the maintenance of disease resistance and a relatively high birth rate. By virtue of these factors, some tribes began to increase in numbers, contrary to the general Native American population trend.

Once the international political situation had stabilized in North America, the United States, Canada, and Mexico proceeded to "pacify" their tribal inhabitants. Colonial warfare then ceased to generate mortality (although a period of frequent direct confrontation between national armed forces and tribesmen long exacted a high toll of the latter). Peace eventually ended the loss of Native Americans in war, until the United States and Canada entered international wars outside the continent and recruited Native Americans to fight in them. National economic consolidation also opened the way to economic imperialism among post-tribal survivors; in time it brought them into the system as wage earners, but seldom as entrepreneurs.

Most important, the long years of colonial contact

between Europeans and Native American peoples generated frequent sexual liaisons between members of the various ethnic groups. Europeans and tribesmen captured members of opposing groups to keep as slaves or concubines (and, at times, to mold into respected citizens). On the social frontier, those disenchanted with their native societies freely mingled and intermarried. Consequently, there now exists a "New American Race," consisting of individuals whose genes came originally from Europe, North America, and Africa. Their cultural allegiance may be national or ethnic.

In the absence of an adequate introductory synthesis of historic demography in North America, some useful perspectives can be gained from the approaches a few outstanding analysts have taken. Nicolás Sánchez-Albornoz has written the best synthesis of trends south of the United States, *The Population of Latin America: A History* [170]. Even in translation, his text reads well. His analysis of aboriginal population size on the eve of conquest and its collapse under European onslaughts is competent and interesting.

Alfred W. Crosby's excellent *The Columbian Exchange: Biological and Cultural Consequences of 1492* [73] provides an exciting introduction to the world-wide transformations produced by the interchange of cultural and biological elements between the Old and New Worlds.

Anthropologists may pride themselves on the application of comparative analytical methods, but two historians have written the best comparisons of the impact of English-speaking and other European peoples on indigenous overseas populations. In "America as a Model" Woodrow W. Borah [15] found that Europeans produced depopulation of the Pacific Islands (including aboriginal Australia) and Africa; from the latter, the slave trade removed 50,000,000 persons. In contrast, European economic policies had little apparent negative effect on Asian population. In fact, New World food crops allowed the Chinese to triple their numbers between 1650 and 1850. In "The Fatal Confrontation: Early Native–White Relations on the Frontiers of Australia, New Guinea, and America—A Comparative Study" Wilbur R. Jacobs [117] very clearly noted the racist basis of English-speaking colonialism in all three areas. Secularizing values and formidable geographic and disease obstacles to European settlement in New Guinea mitigated European impact there.

The fullest exposition of methodological procedures for historical demographic analysis of Spanish colonial areas appears with abundant data in the two volumes of *Essays in Population History, Mexico and the Caribbean* by Cook and Borah [66, 67]. These prolific students of historic American population trends have written far more on the subject than other authors, and their works are fundamental.

Peopling the Continent

Demographers accustomed to analyzing census data

the Tehuacan Valley of Mexico" by Richard S. MacNeish [143] offers the most complete reconstruction of trends in one area. Starting at a density of a half or quarter person per 100 km² from 10,000 to 7,000 B.C., densities rose sharply to 0.4 per km² between 1200 and 900 B.C., and peaked at 41.66 per km² after 1500. This evidence is fully persented in *The Prehistory of the Tehuacan Valley* under the general editorship of Douglas S. Byers [25].

The widest-ranging such reconstruction is William T. Sanders's "Population, Agricultural History, and Societal Evolution in Mesoamerica" [172]. Sanders claimed that the Mexican central basin population rose steadily (with migration between localities) from about 600 B.C. to A.D. 700, leveled off until around A.D. 1000, and rapidly increased until contact. He also concluded that Mayan population suffered a major decline after A.D. 100 to between 750,000 and 800,000 at Conquest in Yucatan-Quintana Roo-Campeche.

Proto-historic Population

The size of the immediately pre-Columbian population of North America will never be known with a precision satisfying to all students of the question. Statistics of a quality likely to satisfy everyone simply do not exist. Perhaps the largest "estimate" as to the elusive number is the 16,000,000 to 17,000,000 given by Emmanuel H. Domenech in his 1860 *Seven Years Residence in the Great Deserts of North America* [81]. While Domenech attributed

Forest Civilizations" [28], claiming that in both areas economically undifferentiated peoples exported food surpluses because of their small numbers, not high productivity. Ursula M. Cowgill reported "An Agricultural Study of the Southern Maya Lowlands" [71] which rejects the notion that field-invading grass limited slash-and-burn cultivation. She concluded that Mayan techniques could support 38 to 77 persons per km^2; thus, historic density runs a hundreth of their horticultural carrying capacity. B. L. Turner reported raised fields and terraces in "Prehistoric Intensive Agriculture in the Mayan Lowlands" [198] to show that prehistoric Mayans were not limited to slash-and-burn production and could reach population densities of 150 per km^2 by cultivating three-fourths of the land.

Farther north in Mesoamerica, Don E. Dumond analyzed the "Demographic Aspects of the Classic Period in Puebla-Tlaxcala" [85]. From a 500,000 population in 1519, Dumond calculated 100,000 inhabitants about 100 B.C., doubling in 700 years. His technique of comparing numbers of prehistoric settlements from different times illuminates trends, whatever specific figures may be. Sherburne F. Cook and Adan E. Treganza pioneered this estimation technique from site size in *The Quantitative Investigation of Indian Mounds* [69]. Raoul Naroll refined it to one person per 10 m^2 of floor area in "Floor Area and Settlement Population" [156].

"Social Implications of Changes in Population and Settlement Pattern of the 12,000 Years of Prehistory in and improved enumeration in *Indian Population in the United States and Alaska, 1910* [204]. The total rose to 332,397 in 1930, according to the Bureau of the Census in *The Indian Population of the United States and Alaska; Fifteenth Census of the United States: 1930* [205].

When the 1960 census reported by "census county divisions," George A. Hillery, Jr. and Frank J. Essene carried out "Navajo Population: an Analysis of the 1960 Census" [110]. They estimated 54,700 reservation residents, stressing household sizes double the Anglo average and fertility higher than that in rural Latin America.

The most striking change in the Native American demographic pattern is rapid urbanization as seen in *Census of Population: 1970; Subject Reports. Final Report PC(2)-1F American Indians* [206]. By 1970, the enumerated Native American population was 44.6% urban, and only 6.2% rural farm-dwelling. Outside of the Navajo Reservation, the Los Angeles Standard Metropolitan Statistical Area (SMSA) contained more Native American inhabitants than any other locale (23,908), followed by Tulsa (15,182); Oklahoma City (12,951); San Francisco–Oakland (12,041); Phoenix (10,127); Minneapolis–Saint Paul (9,911); New York (9,984); Seattle–Everett (8,814); and Tucson (8,704). Only the Pine Ridge Sioux Reservation's 8,280 Native Americans outnumbered the Indian population enumerated in Chicago (8,203); in San Diego (6,007); and in the San Bernardino–Riverside–Ontario SMSA (5,941).

Since 1955, the United States Public Health Service

has been responsible for the maintenance of Native American health throughout the nation, and has carried out many analyses of reservation population and the factors affecting it. Unfortunately, these studies are typically reported only in mimeographed form.

For Canada, Diamond Jenness's *The Indians of Canada* [120] places 1924 census returns in historic perspective. Anatol Romaniuk and Victor L. Piché's "Natality Estimates for the Canadian Indians by Stable Population Models, 1900–1969" [167] shows that both the national census and the Department of Indian Affairs had underenumerated Indians prior to about 1960, though the Native American population of Canada increased from at least 1900 until 1960 with birth rates sometimes over 44 per 1,000 and falling death rates during that time span. In other words, the analysis of Native American — Indian and Eskimo — population trends in Canada appears to have been quite neglected.

Any reader who might have persevered in perusing this evaluation of works dealing with Native American population will have formed an impression of their characteristics. The works discussed are extremely diverse in both form and origin, even when they do not treat population trends as secondary to analysis of other subjects. Historians, anthropologists, medical researchers, and one outstanding physiologist wrote most of what the author considers to be significant contributions. These scholarly disciplines are not exactly noted for their conceptual communication one with another, so one should not express suprise at finding dissimilarities in their population research.

Disciplinary differences between research reports merely emphasize that most discussions of Native American population are fairly technical in nature. The subject has attracted only a handful of synthesizers and no popularizer. As a consequence, recommending an entry-point into this literature for the beginner without any knowledge of the matter would be next to impossible were it not for one truly fine book. Anyone wishing to increase his comprehension of the world in which we live can benefit from reading Alfred Crosby's *The Columbian Exchange* [73]. After that, the present essay hopefully provides a useful chart for navigating in unfamiliar intellectual waters.

Recommended Works

For the Beginner

[15] Woodrow W. Borah, "America As Model."

[66, 67] Sherburne F. Cook and Woodrow W. Borah, *Essays in Population History, Mexico and the Caribbean.*

[73] Alfred W. Crosby, Jr., *The Columbian Exchange.*

[117] Wilbur R. Jacobs, "The Fatal Confrontation."

For a Basic Library Collection

[6] Homer Aschmann, *The Central Desert of Baja California.*

[9] Martin A. Baumhoff, *Ecological Determinants of Aboriginal California Populations.*

Woodrow W. Borah and Sherburne F. Cook.

[18] *The Population of Central Mexico in 1548.*

[19] *The Aboriginal Population of Central Mexico on the Eve of the Spanish Conquest.*

Sherburne F. Cook.

[31] *The Extent and Significance of Disease among the Indians of Baja California, 1770–1845.*

[34] *Population Trends Among the California Mission Indians.*

[36, 37, 38, 39] *The Conflict Between the California Indian and White Civilization.*

[48] *Soil Erosion and Population in Central Mexico.*

[49] *The Aboriginal Population of the San Joaquin Valley, California.*

[50] *The Epidemic of 1830–1833 in California and Oregon.*

[51] *The Aboriginal Population of the North Coast of California.*

[52] *The Aboriginal Population of Alameda and Contra Costa Counties, California.*

[55] *Erosion Morphology and Occupation History in Western Mexico.*

Sherburne F. Cook and Woodrow W. Borah.

[63] *The Indian Population of Central Mexico, 1531–1610.*

[65] *The Population of the Mixteca Alta, 1520–1960.*

[70] Donald B. Cooper, *Epidemic Disease in Mexico City, 1761–1813.*

[73] Alfred W. Crosby, Jr., *The Columbian Exchange.*

[84] John Duffy, *Epidemics in Colonial America.*

Carl O. Sauer.

[173] *Aboriginal Population of Northwestern Mexico.*

[174] *Colima of New Spain in the Sixteenth Century.*

[184] Esther A. and Allen E. Stearn, *The Effect of Smallpox on the Destiny if the Amerindian.*

[201] Douglas H. Ubelaker, *Reconstruction of Demographic Profiles.*

Bibliographical List

*Denotes items suitable for secondary school students

[1] Aberle, Sophie B. D. 1931. "Frequency of Pregnancies and Birth Interval Among Pueblo Indians." *American Journal of Physical Anthropology* 16:63–80.

[2] Aberle, Sophie B.; Watkins, J. H.; and Pitney, E. H. 1940. "The Vital History of San Juan Pueblo." *Human Biology* 12:141–87.

[3] Adams, Morton S.; Brown, Kenneth S.; Iba, Barbara Y.; and Niswander, Jerry D. 1970. "Health of Papago Indian Children." *Public Health Reports* 85:1047–61.

[4] Alvarado, Anita L. 1970. "Cultural Determinants of Population Stability in the Havasupai Indians." *American Journal of Physical Anthropology* 33:9–14.

[5] Archibald, William S. and Kunitz, Stephen J. 1971. "Detection of Plague by Testing Serum of Dogs on the Navajo Reservation." *Health Service and Mental Health Administration Reports* 86:377–80.

[6] Aschmann, Homer. 1959. *The Central Desert of Baja California: Demography and Ecology.* Ibero-Americana:42. Berkeley: University of California Press.

[7] Ashburn, Percy M. 1947. *The Ranks of Death, A Medical History of the Conquest of America,* ed. Frank D. Ashburn. New York: Coward-McCann.

Baumhoff, Martin A.

[8] 1958. *California Athabascan Groups.* Anthropological Records:16, pt. 5, pp. 157–237. Berkeley: University of California Press.

[9] 1963. *Ecological Determinants of Aboriginal California Populations.* University of California Publications in American Archaeology and Ethnology:49, pt. 2, pp. 155–236. Berkeley: University of California Press.

[10] Bennett, Peter H.; Burch, Thomas A.; and Miller, Max. 1971. "Diabetes mellitus in American (Pima) Indians." *Lancet* 11:125–28.

[11] Bennett, Peter H.; Steinberg, Arthur G.; Miller, Max; and Burch, Thomas A. 1965. "Effect of aging on the glucose tolerance test: Evidence that the normal standards change only slightly with age." *Journal of Laboratory and Clinical Medicine* 66:852-53.

[12] Bishop, Charles Aldrich. 1974. *The Northern Ojibwa and the Fur Trade: An Historical and Ecological Study.* Toronto: Holt, Rinehart and Winston of Canada.

Borah, Woodrow Wilson.

[13] 1951. *New Spain's Century of Depression.* Ibero-Americana:35. Berkeley: University of California Press.

[14] 1962. "Population Decline and the Social and Institutional Changes of New Spain in the Middle Decades of the Sixteenth Century." In *Akten des 34 Internationalen Amerikanisten kongresses, Wien, 1960,* pp. 172-78. Horn-Wien: Ferdinand Berger.

[15] 1964. "American As Model: The Demographic Impact of European Expansion Upon the Non-European World." In *Actas y Memorias, XXXV Congreso Internacional de Americanistas, Mexico, 1962,* 3 vols., vol. 3, pp. 379-87. Mexico: Editorial Libros de Mexico.

[16] 1970. "The California Mission." In *Ethnic Conflict in California History*, comp. Charles Wollenberg, pp. 1–22. Los Angeles: Tinnon–Brown Inc.

[17] 1970. "The Historical Demography of Latin America: Sources, Techniques, Controversies, Yields." In *Population and Economics, Proceedings of Section V (Historical Demography) of the Fourth Congress of the International Economic History Association . . . 1968*, ed. Paul Deprez, pp. 173–205. Winnipeg: University of Manitoba Press.

Borah, Woodrow Wilson and Cook, Sherburne Friend.

[18] 1960. *The Population of Central Mexico in 1548*. Ibero-Americana:43. Berkeley: University of California Press.

[19] 1963. *The Aboriginal Population of Central Mexico on the Eve of the Spanish Conquest*. Ibero-Americana:45. Berkeley: University of California Press.

[20] 1967. "New Demographic Research on the Sixteenth Century in Mexico." In *Latin American History: Essays on Its Study and Teaching, 1898–1965*, comp. and ed. Howard F. Cline, 2 vols., vol. 2 (1946–65), pp. 717–22. Austin: University of Texas Press.

[21]   1969. "Conquest and Population: A Demographic Approach to Mexican History." *American Philosophical Society, Proceedings* 113:177-83.

[22]   Boyd, Mark Frederick; Smith, Hale G.; and Griffin, John W. 1951. *Here They Once Stood; the Tragic End of the Apalachee Missions.* Gainesville: University of Florida Press.

[23]   Brading, D. A. and Wu, Celia. 1973. "Population Growth and Crisis: León, 1720-1860." *Journal of Latin American Studies* 5:1-36.

[24]   Brown, R. Chris; Gurunanjappa, Bale S.; Hawk, Rodney J.; and Bitsuie, Delphine. 1970. "The Epidemiology of Accidents Among the Navajo Indians." *Public Health Reports* 85:881-88.

[25]   Byers, Douglas S., gen. ed. 1967- . *The Prehistory of the Tehuacan Valley.* 5 vols. Austin: For the Robert S. Peabody Foundation, Phillips Academy, Andover, [by the] University of Texas Press.

[26]   Chittenden, Hiram Martin. 1902. *The American Fur Trade of the Far West* . . . 3 vols. New York, F. P. Harper. (Reprinted, 3 vols. in 2, Stanford: Academic Reprints, 1954.)

[27]   Clements, Forrest. 1931. "Racial Differences in Mortality and Morbidity." *Human Biology* 3:397-419.

[28] Coe, Michael D. 1961. "Social Typology and the Tropical Forest Civilizations." *Comparative Studies in Society and History* 4:65–85.

Cook, Sherburne Friend.

[29] 1935. "Diseases of the Indians of Lower California in the Eighteenth Century." *California and Western Medicine* 43:432–34.

[30] 1936. "California's First Medical Survey: Report of Surgeon-General José Benites." *California and Western Medicine* 45:352–54.

[31] 1937. *The Extent and Significance of Disease among the Indians of Baja California, 1697–1773.* Ibero-Americana:12. Berkeley: University of California Press.

[32] 1939. "Smallpox in Spanish and Mexican California, 1770–1845." *Bulletin of the History of Medicine* 7:153–91.

[33] 1939. "The Smallpox Epidemic of 1797 in Mexico." *Bulletin of the History of Medicine* 7:937–69.

[34] 1940. *Population Trends Among the California Mission Indians.* Ibero-Americana:17. Berkeley: University of California Press.

[35] 1941. "Francisco Xavier Balmis and the Introduction of Vaccination to Latin America." *Bulletin of the History of Medicine* 11:543–60 and 12:70–101.

[36]   1943. *The Conflict Between the California Indian and White Civilization: I. The Indian Versus the Spanish Mission.* Ibero-Americana: 21. Berkeley: University of California Press.

[37]   1943. *The Conflict Between the California Indian and White Civilization: II. The Physical and Demographic Reaction of the Nonmission Indians in Colonial and Provincial California.* Ibero-Americana:22. Berkeley: University of California Press.

[38]   1943. *The Conflict Between the California Indian and White Civilization: III. The American Invasion, 1848–1870.* Ibero-Americana:23. Berkeley: University of California Press.

[39]   1943. *The Conflict Between the California Indian and White Civilization. IV. Trends in Marriage and Divorce Since 1850.* Ibero-Americana:24. Berkeley: University of California Press.

[40]   1943. "Migration and Urbanization of the Indians of California." *Human Biology* 15:33–45.

[41]   1943. "Racial Fusion among the California and Nevada Indians." *Human Biology* 15:153–65.

[42]   1945. "Demographic Consequences of European Contact with Primitive Peoples." *Annals of the American Academy of Political and Social Science* 237:107–11.

[43] 1946. "Human Sacrifice and Warfare as Factors in the Demography of Pre-colonial Mexico." *Human Biology* 18:81–102.

[44] 1946. "The Incidence and Significance of Disease among the Aztecs and Related Tribes." *Hispanic American Historical Review* 26:320–35.

[45] 1947. "The Interrelation of Population, Food Supply and Building in Pre-conquest Central Mexico." *American Antiquity* 13:45–52.

[46] 1947. "Survivorship in Aboriginal Populations." *Human Biology* 19:83–89.

[47] 1949. *The Historical Demography and Ecology of the Teotlapan.* Ibero-Americana:33. Berkeley: University of California Press.

[48] 1949. *Soil Erosion and Population in Central Mexico.* Ibero-Americana:34. Berkeley: University of California Press.

[49] 1955. *The Aboriginal Population of the San Joaquin Valley, California.* Anthropological Records:16, pt. 2, pp. 31–80. Berkeley: University of California Press.

[50] 1955. *The Epidemic of 1830–1833 in California and Oregon.* University of California Publications in American Archaeology and Ethnology:43, pt. 3, pp. 303–26. Berkeley: University of California Press.

[51]   1956. *The Aboriginal Population of the North Coast of California.* Anthropological Records:16, pt. 3, pp. 81–128. Berkeley: University of California Press.

[52]   1957. *The Aboriginal Population of Alameda and Contra Costa Counties, California.* Anthropological Records:16, pt. 4, pp. 131–55. Berkeley: University of California Press.

[53]   1958. *Santa Maria Ixcatlán: Habitat, Population, Subsistence.* Ibero-Americana:41. Berkeley: University of California Press.

[54]   1960. "Reconstruction of Extinct Populations." *Revista Mexicana de Estudios Antropológicos* 16:173–82.

[55]   1963. *Erosion Morphology and Occupation History in Western Mexico.* Anthropological Records:17, pt. 3, pp. 281–334. Berkeley: University of California Press.

[56]   1964. "The Aboriginal Population of Upper California." In *Actas y Memorias, XXXV Congreso Internacional de Americanistas, Mexico, 1962,* 3 vols., vol. 3, pp. 397–403. Mexico: Editorial Libros de Mexico.

[57]   1968. "The Destruction of the California Indians." *California Alumni Monthly* (Dec.) 79:14–19.

[58] 1970. "The California Indian and Anglo-American Culture." In *Ethnic Conflict in California History,* comp. Charles Wollenberg, pp. 23–42. See [16].

[59] 1970. "Migration as a Factor in the History of Mexican Population: Sample Data from West Central Mexico, 1793–1950." In *Population and Economics,* ed. Paul Deprez, pp. 279–302. See [17].

[60] 1973. "Interracial Warfare and Population Decline among the New England Indians." *Ethnohistory* 20:1–24.

[61] 1973. "The Significance of Disease in the Extinction of the New England Indians." *Human Biology* 45:485–508.

Cook, Sherburne Friend and Borah, Woodrow Wilson.

[62] 1957. "The Rate of Population Change in Central Mexico, 1550–1570." *Hispanic American Historical Review* 37:463–70.

[63] 1960 *The Indian Population of Central Mexico, 1531–1610.* Ibero-Americana:44. Berkeley: University of California Press.

[64] 1966. "On the Credibility of Contemporary Testimony on the Population of Mexico in the Sixteenth Century." In *Summa anthropológica en*

homenaje a Roberto J. Weitlaner, pp. 229-39. Mexico: Instituto Nacional de Antropología e Historia, Secretaria de Educación Púbica.

[65] 1968. *The Population of the Mixteca Alta, 1520-1960.* Ibero-Americana:50. Berkeley: University of California Press.

[66] 1971. *Essays in Population History, Mexico and the Caribbean, Volume I.* Berkeley: University of California Press.

[67] 1974. *Essays in Population History: Mexico and the Caribbean, Volume II.* Berkeley: University of California Press.

[68] Cook, Sherburne Friend and Simpson, Leslie Byrd. 1948. *The Population of Central Mexico in the Sixteenth Century.* Ibero-Americana:31. Berkeley: University of California Press.

[69] Cook, Sherburne Friend and Treganza, Adan Eduardo. 1950. *The Quantitative Investigation of Indian Mounds.* University of California Publications in American Archaeology and Ethnology:40, pt. 5, pp. 223-61. Berkeley: University of California Press.

[70] Cooper, Donald B. 1965. *Epidemic Disease in Mexico City, 1761-1813: An Administrative, Social, and Medical Study.* Austin: University of Texas Press, published for the Institute of Latin American Studies.

[71] Cowgill, Ursula M. 1962. "An Agricultural Study of the Southern Maya Lowlands." *American Anthropologist* 64:273–86.

Crosby, Alfred W., Jr.

[72] 1967. "Conquistador y Pestilencia: The First New World Pandemic and the Fall of the Great Indian Empires." *Hispanic American Historical Review* 47:321–37.

*[73] 1972. *The Columbian Exchange: Biological and Cultural Consequences of 1492.* Westport, Conn.: Greenwood Pub. Co.

[74] Deagan, Kathleen A. 1973. "*Mestizaje* in Colonial San Augustine." *Ethnohistory* 20:55–65.

Dobyns, Henry F.

[75] 1951. *Papagos in the Cotton Fields, 1950.* Tucson: The Author, for the Arizona State Museum.

[76] 1962. *Pioneering Christians Among the Perishing Indians of Tucson.* Lima: Editorial Estudios Andinos.

[77] 1963. "Indian Extinction in the Middle Santa Cruz River Valley, Arizona." *New Mexico Historical Review* 38:163–81.

[78] 1966. "Estimating Aboriginal American Population: An Appraisal of Techniques with a New Hemispheric Estimate." *Current Anthropology* 7:395–416 and "Reply," 440–44.

[79] 1976. *Spanish Colonial Tucson: A Demographic History.* Tucson: University of Arizona Press.

[80] Doeblin, Thomas D.; Evans, Kathleen; Ingall, Gillian B.; Dowling, Kathleen; Chilcote, Elsa W.; and Bannerman, Robin M. 1969. "Diabetes and Hyperglycemia in Seneca Indians." *Human Heredity* 19:613–27.

[81] Domenech, Emmanuel Henri Dieudonné. 1860. *Seven Years Residence in the Great Deserts of North America.* London: Longman, Green, Longman and Roberts.

*[82] Dozier, Edward P. 1966. "Problem Drinking Among American Indians: The Role of Sociocultural Deprivation." *Quarterly Journal of Studies on Alcohol* 27:72–87.

Duffy, John.

[83] 1951. "Smallpox and the Indians in the American Colonies." *Bulletin of the History of Medicine* 25:324–41.

[84] 1953. *Epidemics in Colonial America.* Baton Rouge: Louisiana State University Press. (Reprinted, Port Washington, N. Y.: Kennikat Press, 1972.)

[85] Dumond, Don E. 1972. "Demographic Aspects of the Classic Period in Puebla-Tlaxcala." *Southwestern Journal of Anthropology* 28:101–30.

[86] Elston, R. C.; Namboodiri, K. K.; Nino, H. V.; and Pollitzer, W. S. 1974. "Studies on Blood and Urine Glucose in Seminole Indians: Indications for Segregation of a Major Gene." *American Journal of Human Genetics* 26:13–34.

*[87] Ewers, John C. 1973. "The Influence of Epidemics on the Indian Population and Cultures of Texas." *Plains Anthropoligist* 18:104–15.

[88] Fenna, Donald, Mix, Lawrence; Schaefer, Otto; and Gilbert, James A. L. 1971. "Ethanol Metabolism in Various Racial Groups." *Canadian Medical Association Journal* 105:472–75.

[89] Ferguson, Frances Nocthend. 1968. "Navaho Drinking: Some Tentative Hypotheses." *Human Organization* 27:159–67.

[90] Gilbert, William Harlen, Jr. 1948. "Surviving Indian Groups of the Eastern United States." In *Smithsonian Institution Annual Report for 1948*, pp. 407–38. Washington, D.C.: U. S. Government Printing Office.

[91] Glassner, Martin Ira. 1974. "Population Figures for Mandan Indians." *The Indian Historian* (Spring) 7:41–46.

Gold, Robert L.

[92] 1965. "The Settlement of the Pensacola Indians in New Spain, 1763–1770." *Hispanic American*

Historical Review 45:567-76.

[93] 1969. *Borderland Empires in Transition: The Triple-Nation Transfer of Florida.* Carbondale: Southern Illinois University Press.

[94] González Navarro, Moisés. 1970. "*Mestizaje* in Mexico During the National Period." In *Race and Class in Latin America,* ed. Magnus Mörner, pp. 145-69. New York: Columbia University Press.

[95] Graves, Theodore D. 1967. "Acculturation, Access and Alcohol in a Tri-Ethnic Community." *American Anthropologist* 69:306-21.

[96] Greene, Evarts Boutell and Harrington, Virginia D. 1932. *American Population Before the Federal Census of 1790.* New York: Columbia University Press.

Hackenberg, Robert Allan.

[97] 1961. *Papago Population Study: Research Methods and Preliminary Results . . .* Tucson: Bureau of Ethnic Research, Department of Anthropology, University of Arizona.

[98] 1966. "An Anthropological Study of Demographic Transition: The Papago Information System." *Milbank Memorial Fund Quarterly* 44: 470-93.

birds and animals. The horticultural Mayan civilization that once flourished in the tropical areas of southern Mexico, Guatemala, and Honduras holds a special fascination for New World prehistorians. Counting house mounds, Oliver G. and Edith B. Ricketson estimated 271 inhabitants per mi.² in *Uaxactun, Guatemala. Group E — 1926–1931* [166]. In "The Density of Population in the Southern and Northern Mayan Empires as an Archaeological and Geographical Problem" Franz Termer [194] projected modern settlement sizes back in time, allowing a 50% decrease since Conquest to estimate 500,000 inhabitants in late prehistory — a density of only 3.7 per km². Joseph A. Hester put km² density nearer 30 in "Agriculture, Economy and Population Densities of the Maya." [109] William T. Sanders placed density at about 20 persons per km² in "The Anthropogeography of Central Veracruz" [171], although he calculated 35 per km² farther north. Slyvanus G. Morley and George W. Brainerd in *The Ancient Maya* [152] considered field-invading grass a limiting factor, calculating densities of 68 or 136 persons per mi.² by assuming less simultaneous occupation than had the Ricketsons.

Robert F. Heizer in "Agriculture and the Theocratic State in Lowland Southeastern Mexico" [107] hypothesized that slash-and-burn horticulturalists (living 20 per km² as early as 800 to 400 B.C.) could have easily constructed the massive La Venta site Olmec period pyramid and mounds. Michael D. Coe compared Maya to Cambodia in "Social Typology and the Tropical will be little satisfied with the quality of information necessarily utilized in historical demography of the New World. The scientific attitude of historians, anthropologists, and human biologists dealing with the matter is eloquently summed up in Cook's methodological statement on "Reconstruction of Extinct Populations" [54]. One either uses such data as may be available and learns something, however inadequate, or abjures such data and learns nothing. Analyzing North American archaeological and California historical data in "Survivorship in Aboriginal Populations," Cook [46] countered claims of genetic determinism, demonstrating that tribal peoples react to their environments as do large-scale civilized populations.

T. Dale Stewart succinctly summarized current theory about the peopling of the Americas from Siberia across a glacial-age land connection where the Bering Strait lies now and reviewed historic assumptions about Native American origins. Ranging over a hemisphere in *The People of America,* Stewart [187] touched upon many topics, including the size of pre-Columbian population, its intestinal parasites, and probable freedom from such diseases as malaria, syphilis, and tuberculosis. Perhaps the best summation of archeological evidence for Paleo-Indian expansion across the continent appears in "The Discovery of America" by Paul S. Martin [146].

Most Native American population growth occurred after descendants of the big-game hunting colonizers learned to cultivate food plants and to domesticate a few a loss of 12,000,000 Indians to wars and maladies, his identification of the 1837 smallpox epidemic as the first introduced by Whites clearly reveals his figures to have been sheer supposition based upon very minimal knowledge of actual historic processes.

A pioneer attempt to arrive at a continental figure from archeological evidence was Herbert J. Spinden's 1928 "The Population of Ancient America" [182]. Spinden estimated 50,000,000 to 75,000,000 Native Americans in A.D. 1200, arguing that abundant, large mounds in midcontinental river valleys meant that those horticultural areas must have once supported several million inhabitants.

James Mooney's estimates of Indian population were long accorded the most influence. His brief 1910 "Population" [150] gives 1,150,000 as the total north of Mexico at the arrival of Europeans, with 846,000 in the United States, 220,000 in British America, and 72,000 in Alaska. In *The Aboriginal Population of America North of Mexico* posthumously issued in 1928, Mooney [151] compiled tribe-by-tribe estimates at varied times. Alfred L. Kroeber re-estimated "Native American Population" in 1934 [126] and in his 1939 ambitious *Cultural and Natural Areas of Native North America* [127]. He accepted Mooney's compilation except for California, so reduced the continental total to 1,025,950 or 900,000 north of the Río Grande. Kroeber estimated 8,400,000 aboriginal Native Americans in the Western Hemisphere prior to European impact. In his state-by-state summary of *The Indian*

Tribes of North America John R. Swanton [189] continued the pattern of compiling tribal estimates with minimal analysis.

A long, painstaking reconstruction of central Mexican population by Cook and Borah led the latter in "America as Model: The Demographic Impact of European Expansion upon the Non-European World" [15] to suggest that 100,000,000 Native Americans lived at the end of the fifteenth century. Dobyns in "Estimating Aboriginal American Population: An Appraisal of the Techniques with a New Hemispheric Estimate" [78] condemned the estimates of Mooney and Kroeber, citing faulty methodology, and approved of those practices employed by Cook and Borah as yielding more accurate results. Dobyns estimated from 90,000,000 to 112,000,000 pre-Columbian Native Americans, using two different depopulation ratios and historic enumerations.

These drastic revisions spread to historians through such essays as Wilbur R. Jacobs's "The Tip of an Iceberg: Pre-Columbian Indian Demography and Some Implications for Revisionism" [118] and Borah's "The Historical Demography of Latin America: Sources, Techniques, Controversies, Yields" [17]. Placing writers in historiographic perspective, Borah identified a "Robertson–Bandelier" tendency to view Native American social structure as simple, their economic surpluses as small, and to postulate small aboriginal populations that grew steadily with historic "progress." He labeled as

"Clavijero–Prescott" the tendency to view Native American social structure as highly complex, surpluses as very large, and population trends as cyclical.

Since Domenech, estimates of native North American numbers have been markedly lower. The historian William C. MacLeod's estimates of North American numbers are much greater than Mooney's in *The American Indian Frontier* [142]. Taking 2,000,000 mi.² of the United States to have been fit for occupation and Kroeber's one person per mi.², MacLeod projected 2,000,000 pre-Columbian inhabitants, with some 3,000,000 on the continent after reckoning the northwest Pacific coast fisheries and the fertility of the Saint Lawrence River valley. A literal interpretation of MacLeod's figures yields a population of 4,000,000.

Homer Aschmann analyzed *The Central Desert of Baja California: Demography and Ecology* [6] and reconstructed a minimum density of 1.12 persons per habitable mi.² or 0.97 for all territory. Density could not have been less in better-watered lands; thus, there could not have been fewer than 2,240,000 pre-Columbians in the United States. Douglas H. Ubelaker achieved an unprecedented *Reconstruction of Demographic Profiles from Ossuary Skeletal Samples: A Case Study from the Tidewater Potomac* [201]. He found skeletal and documentary evidence that the Conoy, a group which Mooney estimated at 2,000, actually numbered from 7,200 to 8,400. The latter total suggests a density of 1.2 persons per km² or half again as much as MacLeod's tidewater Virginia estimate.

By far the best reconstructions of aboriginal population magnitudes and historic Native American depopulation–repopulation yet achieved are the work of Woodrow W. Borah and Sherburne F. Cook for central Mexico. Cook's initial estimate of 2,700,000 central Mexicans stems from his "exploratory" analysis of "The Interrelation of Population, Food Supply and Building in Pre-Conquest Central Mexico" [45]. Analyzing past human use of an area formerly the seat of the Toltec Empire, Cook in *The Historical Demography and Ecology of the Teotlalpan* [47] reported a series of cyclical population trends lasting 400 to 500 years each. Political integration generated population growth; invasion and political disintegration brought depopulation. European conquest may be merely another cycle. Ranging widely to study stream channel cutting and deposition related to slope erosion, Cook in *Soil Erosion and Population in Central Mexico* [48] demonstrated that intensive cultivation by very populous prehistoric Native Americans changed soil far more tham historic land use. Cook extended this analysis in *Erosion Morphology and Occupation History in Western Mexico* [55], emphasizing that gullying reveals locations of prehistoric population concentrations and topsoil loss signifies historic livestock grazing.

Cook identified several kinds of evidence to document that the central Mexican population had outstripped the long-range human carrying capacity of the land. In his 1946 "Human Sacrifice and Warfare as Factors in the Demography of Pre-colonial Mexico" Cook [43] interpreted inter-kingdom warfare and human sacrifice as fifteenth century behavioral responses to overpopulation — although he estimated central Mexican population at only 2,000,000. In "The Incidence and Significance of Disease among the Aztecs and Related Tribes" Cook [44] stressed native resistance to local gastrointestinal ills and the absence of Old World diseases as a result of geographic isolation. Consequently, pre-Columbian population grew until it pressed "close upon the food supply." Saul Jarcho in "Some Observations on Diseases in Prehistoric America" [119] also concluded that pre-Columbian North Americans were free of malaria and yellow fever, but suffered from syphilis.

Cook and Leslie B. Simpson began in 1948 to revise aboriginal population estimates using documentary sources. In *The Population of Central Mexico in the Sixteenth Century* [68] they extrapolated from the reported size of armies to figure 8,950,000 central Mexicans just prior to Conquest. They postulated 11,002,450 by assuming that 4,409,180 people in 1565 (indicated in various reports) constituted 40% of the 1519 population.

Borah and Cook summarized their later work in "New Demographic Research on the Sixteenth Century in Mexico" [20] and in "Conquest and Population: A Demographic Approach to Mexican History" [21]. They agreed upon an estimate of 25,200,000 persons in 1519. Colonial record-keeping of Spanish economic exploitation of Native Americans enabled Cook and Borah to estimate the 1519 population several ways. Borah and

Cook based *The Aboriginal Population of Central Mexico on the Eve of the Spanish Conquest* [19] on the description of tribute assessments of the Triple Alliance prepared at Cortés's orders. Assuming an average 4.5 persons per family, they calculated 25,200,000, or a density of 49 per km². If the family averaged five members prior to the Conquest's disruption, there were 29,000,000 persons, giving a density of 54.5 per km².

Carl O. Sauer calculated the pre-Conquest population of Colima on the west coast as 140,000 minimum in *Colima of New Spain in the Sixteenth Century* [174]. Drawing mainly on a 1550s Spanish inspection, Sauer cited statements such as the discovery of thirty-five male tributaries from various pre-Conquest towns aggregated in a single settlement where the inspector estimated 15,000 tributaries must have been parceled out among twenty-seven conquerors only thirty-two years earlier.

In their first volume of *Essays in Population History, Mexico and the Caribbean* [66] Cook and Borah reconstructed the depopulation and recovery of west-central Mexico from 1548 to 1960. They also presented a refinement of their methods for analyzing demographic history and discussions of family, household, civil category, and age-group structure in colonial Mexico. Their chapter on "The Aboriginal Population of Hispaniola" re-examines early colonial records to define 8,000,000 aboriginal inhabitants as the midpoint of the range of estimation. Because this figure exceeds even the number the reformist Friar Bartolomé de las Casas envisioned as inhabiting the island prior to Spanish conquest, it takes on great historic significance. Their analysis builds upon Sauer's emphasis in *The Early Spanish Main* [175] upon the productivity of aboriginal root–crop horticulture, and a re-assessment of the evidence that Bartholomew Columbus enumerated more than 1,100,000 tribute-payers over 14 years of age on half the island held by the Spaniards in 1496.

In their second volume of *Essays*, Cook and Borah [67] dealt with "The Population of Yucatan 1517–1960," and racial groups, marriage age, birth, fertility, and mortality patterns in Mexico from colonial times to the present. They concluded that the population of Yucatan, isolated by lowland swamps from central Mexico, followed an independent historic course. It peaked in prehistoric Toltec times, falling for a century before the Conquest to 800,000, and then declined to a quarter of the initial contact magnitude. The numbers fell again in the mid-seventeenth century to a mid-eighteenth-century nadir, and grew thereafter until the mid-nineteenth-century War of the Castes caused another decline. The population has since been growing steadily.

Carl O. Sauer first ventured to estimate from early Spanish documents *The Aboriginal Population of Northwestern Mexico* [173]. His 540,000 figure implies a density of 1.7 persons per km^2. While Sauer mentioned severe epidemics, he did not allow for their depopulation. His estimate, therefore, referred to the eve of or just after the Spaniards achieved colonial control, not to pre-epidemic populations. A Jesuit record of over 30,000 Yaquis along 14 leagues of river in 1619 (after serious epidemic mortality in 1617–18, 1611, 1602, 1601 and 1592–93) signifies that about 1590 the Yaquis numbered nearer 60,000 than Sauer's 35,000 "aboriginal" estimate. Such a proportional difference over the entire area translates into approximately 930,000 Native Americans, an average density of 2.9 per km^2.

Because far more analyses of Native American population have been made for California than for any other area, these studies loom large in North American historic demography. Stephen Powers pioneered in an 1872 publication, "The Northen California Indians" [161]. Adding 170,000 salmon fishermen to 1,250,000 wild oat consumers, he calculated population density at 50 per mi.^{2} over 25,000 mi.^{2} Realizing that California Indians did not rely on wild oats, Powers soon re-estimated to 705,000 in terms of salmon waters and acorns in his 1875 paper on "Californian Indian Characteristics" [162]. He refused to revise that figure when his studies were republished in 1877 as "Tribes of California" [162].

C. Hart Merriam employed a different estimation technique in his 1905 view of "The Indian Population of California" [148]. He thought Christian missions held 30,000 souls in 1830; assumed one pagan native per three converts; and added 10,000 for mission period depopulation. Merriam calculated that missions tapped a fifth of the non-desert state and added 10,000 desert-dwellers to arrive at a 260,000 total. In his 1925 *Handbook of California Indians,* Alfred L. Kroeber [125] claimed 24,634 mission Indians in 1830, but rounded to 25,000 and used Merriam's 25% unconverted natives to reach 33,000. He interpolated half of that as post-1769 depopulation to estimate 50,000 pre-Spanish contact Indians in the mission area, but enlarged that area to a third of the state. Kroeber preferred 133,000 aboriginal Californians to the 150,000, giving an average density of 0.433 per km^2 with local maxima of 70 per km^2.

Cook re-estimated *The Aboriginal Population of the San Joaquin Valley, California* [49] in 1955, considering all available Spanish and Mexican information concerning valley tribes. He set aboriginal population at 83,820 — more than four times the 19,000 he concluded had survived in 1851. Cook reviewed earlier estimates of *The Aboriginal Population of the North Coast of California* [51] in 1956. His 70,400 total raised previous figures by from one-sixth to one-third. Then Martin A. Baumhoff calculated aboriginal population from plant food–game–fish resources for *California Athabascan Groups* [8]. Finding an average density of 5 persons per mi.^{2}, Baumhoff raised Cook's total for Athapascan tribes from 17,447 to 18,779, as compared to Kroeber's mere 6,000. This implies that Cook's North Coast total should be in excess of 71,800.

In 1957 Cook reconsidered *The Aboriginal Population of Alameda and Contra Costa Counties, California* [52]. Utilizing descriptions in Spanish travel reports and mission records, he posited 3,000 people in aboriginal times. The results of his last three analyses persuaded Cook that both he and Kroeber had underestimated the number of aboriginal Californians. In "The Aboriginal Population of Upper California" Cook [56] suggested a range from Merriam's 260,000 to 300,000, relying on written records and archeological remains rather than twentieth-century oral tradition.

Baumhoff identified three economic adaptations in *Ecological Determinants of Aboriginal California Populations* [9]. The Lower Klamath fishermen reached a density varying from 2.5 to 10.8 persons per mi.^{2}; acorn gatherer–hunters, 5 in the mountains and 2 in the Central Valley, down to 1 person per 4 mi.^{2} in the high Sierra; but the Sacramento–San Joaquin river fishermen achieved a density of 10 per mi.^{2} Thus, Baumhoff estimated 248,300 Native Americans in these areas and concluded that California could not have held fewer than 350,000 persons prior to European impact.

The fundamental intolerance of early Anglo-Americans toward Native Americans expressed by hunting them and kidnapping their children to work as servants was summarized by Cook in "The Destruction of the California Indians" [57] and in "The California Indians and Anglo-American Culture" [58]. Cook took 250,000 as a reasonable estimate of Native American numbers just before 1769. He put the 1848 Indian population at 125,000 in the northern mountains, 10,000 on the San Joaquin, and 40,000 on the coast south of San Francisco, with fewer than 20,000 left by 1880. Borah also characterized "The California Mission" [16], preferring a pre-1769 estimate of nearly 300,000 Native Americans in California, a density of less than 2 persons per mi.^{2} He calculated that 100,000 died prior to United States annexation, leaving 200,000 Native American tribesmen with 6,000 Spaniards, 4,500 Hispanic individuals, 1,500 Anglo-Americans, and 5,000 Mission Indians.

By the simple expedient of consulting Hudson's Bay Company records of trader censuses or estimates of tribal populations, Herbert C. Taylor, Jr. materially raised Mooney's regional estimates in "Aboriginal Populations of the Lower Northwest Coast" [190]. Although Taylor cut Mooney's Chinook estimate from 22,000 to 5,000, he found evidence of much larger populations in other groups, and estimated 72,300 people in 1780, whereas Mooney supposed 57,600 — a 25% increase.

For the Chipewyan population, H. Paul Thompson succeeded in "Estimating Aboriginal American Population: A Technique Using Anthropological and Biological Data" [196]. Abundant information about caribou enabled him to use tent-making (and historic descriptions of the number of Indians in typical tents) as a means to calculate a minimum population of 4,670 (133% of Mooney's estimate) and a maximum of 10,194, with 6,426 representing the most likely population size.

History of Epidemics

The invasion of New World populations by Old

World pathogens constituted one of the world's greatest biological cataclysms. Relatively little serious study has been directed, however, at the more than sixty serious epidemics recorded among Western Hemisphere Native Americans from the Conquest to 1900.

The best reconstruction of the impact of the initial smallpox pandemic is a chapter in Alfred W. Crosby's *The Columbian Exchange: Biological and Cultural Consequences of 1492* [73], a slight revision of his article "Conquistador y Pestilencia: The First New World Pandemic and the Fall of the Great Indian Empires" [72]. Using evidence recorded in a Mayan dialect, F. Webster McBryde in "Influenza in America During the Sixteenth Century (Guatemala: 1523, 1559–1562, 1576)" [140] argued that influenza afflicted Native Americans in the densely populated regions during the periods indicated. Most later pandemics and epidemics are known only from scattered and brief references to them in colonial and republican chronicles. Accurate professional diagnoses are usually lacking.

Many writers, contemporary and later, mentioned the decimation of coastal New England Native Americans by a "plague" during the years 1616 through 1619. Herbert U. Williams convincingly analyzed historical descriptions to identify it as bubonic plague in "The Epidemic of the Indians of New England 1616–1620, with Remarks on Native American Infections" [209]. Williams doubted that the epidemic produced the 99% mortality estimate given by one colonial writer for the

Massachusetts tribe; yet it so utterly reduced that tribe as to leave productive coasts quite uninhabited.

A major exception to the dearth of studies is the 1779–83 smallpox epidemic. For the New Spain episode, Donald B. Cooper's *Epidemic Disease in Mexico City, 1761–1813* [70] reconstructs (from information in Mexico's national archive) the viceregal perception of the contagion's spread and the measures taken against it. Marc Simmons sketched the impact on Pueblo populations during the Río Grande Valley episode in "New Mexico's Smallpox Epidemic of 1780–1781" [179]. A game shortage complicated recovery of those infected on the Northern Plains because big animals concurrently died off in great numbers, according to Calvin Martin's "Wildlife Diseases as a Factor in the Depopulation of the North American Indian" [145].

Cook used documents in the epidemics branch of the Mexican national archive to reconstruct the course of "The Smallpox Epidemic of 1797 in Mexico" [33]. He ruled out shipboard transmission — blamed by contemporaries — because smallpox cropped up in Campeche in 1793; spread to Veracruz in 1794; Puebla and Tehuantepec in 1795; Oaxaca in 1796; and Mexico City and beyond in 1797, with a 10% case mortality. Inoculation lowered the mean percentage of deaths to 3.5% from 18.5% among unprotected patients. Cooper [70] re-analyzed this epidemic.

From his analysis of wildlife diseases, Martin [145] concluded that a waterborne typhoidal tularemia epidemic struck Ojibwas west of the Great Lakes about 1804, after decimating beavers in 1803.

In *The Epidemic of 1830–1833 in California and Oregon* Cook [50] identified malaria as the killer of three-fourths of the Native Americans then inhabiting the Sacramento and northern San Joaquin valleys and the lower Columbia River banks. H. H. Stage and C. M. Gjullin in "Anopheles and Malaria in the Pacific Northwest" [183] so identified the epidemic without attempting to quantify mortality. Edward W. Twitchell in "The California Pandemic of 1833" [199] called attention to Sacramento–San Joaquin valley mortality without identifying the disease. Ignoring these analyses, Herbert C. Taylor, Jr. and Lester L. Hoaglin, Jr. concluded that "The 'Intermittent Fever' Epidemic of the 1830's on the Lower Columbia River" [191] was an episode of a world-wide viral influenza pandemic that began in China in 1827.

A brief chapter on "The Smallpox Scourge of 1837" in Hiram M. Chittenden's *The American Fur Trade of the Far West* [26] summarizes a northern Great Plains epidemic episode Americanists cannot ignore. Milo M. Quaife edited Francis Chardon's trader's journal, noting Mandan near extinction in "The Smallpox Epidemic on the Upper Missouri" [163].

Frequently, medical historians chronicle the occurrences of epidemic episodes of various diseases among several tribal peoples at different times. Thus, a long chapter on "Epidemic Sickness and Mortality in the English Colonies in North America from Its Earliest Discovery to the Year 1800" in *History of Medicine in the United States* by Francis R. Packard [160] brings together widely dispersed references to several epidemics of smallpox, plague, measles, scarlet fever, influenza, diphtheria, dysentery, and especially yellow fever. Esther W. and Allen E. Stearn summarized scattered sources century-by-century in assessing *The Effect of Smallpox on the Destiny of the Amerindian* [184]. Their otherwise fine analysis seriously underestimates depopulation because it generally follows Mooney's figures. *The Ranks of Death: A Medical History of the Conquest of America* by Percy M. Ashburn and edited by Frank D. Ashburn [7] couches the onslaught of Old World disease agents in military campaign terms. Ashburn exhibited more interest in smallpox, measles, typhus fever, malaria, yellow fever, tuberculosis, dysentery, hookworm, and syphilis than other ills, but tried to assess them all. In "Smallpox and the Indians of the American Colonies" John Duffy [83] similarly summarized diffuse evidence of many epidemics. Duffy's *Epidemics in Colonial America* [84] also refers to epidemic episodes among Native Americans. Of the same genre is Morris E. Leikind's much shorter "Colonial Epidemic Diseases" [135].

Endemic Diseases, Warfare, and Famine

Cook and Borah in "The Rate of Population Change in Central Mexico 1550–1570" [62] produced the best documented single analysis of historic endemic disease impact. They found a 3.8% annual population decline among central Mexicans during twenty years without an epidemic. George C. Shattuck's *The Peninsula of Yucatan: Medical, Biological, Meteorological and Sociological Studies* [178] constitutes a monumental and model exploration of contemporary epidemiology within a historic perspective.

Medical researchers have in recent years begun to study several diseases still endemic among reservation residents, with a view to reducing their mortality. For example, William S. Archibald and Stephen J. Kunitz worked out "Detection of Plague by Testing Serum of Dogs on the Navajo Reservation" [5] as an "early warning" technique. William E. Woodward and his collaborators studied "Acute Diarrhea on an Apache Indian Reservation" [215], finding that this illness afflicted children under four years of age — a majority of them from households lacking either an indoor toilet, water piped indoors, or a refrigerator. Among Fort Apache Reservation children born after 1 January 1969, 37% of the total mortality stemmed from diarrhea. In a densely settled Pueblo environment, William Lasersohn found that "Acute Diarrheal Diseases in a Zuñi Community" [134] produced 4% of all hospital visits; 30% of those examined required hospitalization. Alfred Rubenstein, et al. investigated the "Effect of Improved Sanitary Facilities on Infant Diarrhea in a Hopi Village" [168]. After a 1964 installation of indoor plumbing in the Hopi

Village of Upper Moenkopi, diarrhea admissions of its infants dropped to half the Lower Moenkopi rate. The culturally conservative inhabitants of Lower Moenkopi rejected the sewage disposal system and continued to rely on outdoor water taps and privies.

Studies of several contemporary reservation populations reveal a prevalence of diabetes far exceeding that among the general population. In "Diabetes mellitus: a 'Thrifty' Genotype Rendered Detrimental by 'Progress'?" James V. Neel [157] theorized that a fat-storage mechanism was adaptive for hunting–gathering populations eating little carbohydrate, but became deleterious when they shifted to domesticated foodstuffs rich in carbohydrates and lessened their physical activity. Very recent epidemiological studies and animal experiments suggest that viral diseases damaging the islets of Langerhans in the pancreas cause diabetes in genetically susceptible individuals. Whatever the mechanism, most Native Americans studied suffer glucose-challenge defined hyperglycemia — an operational definition of diabetes — from 50% greater than to seven times the 2% national diabetes rate.

Eskimos appear, on the other hand, to suffer a diabetes rate half that of the general population. Moreover, when George J. Mouratoff, et al. screened for "Diabetes mellitus in Athabascan Indians in Alaska" [154], they discovered only a 1.6% incidence of high blood glucose two hours after challenge.

Elsewhere, prevalence rates are grim. Thomas D.

Doeblin, et al. found "Diabetes and Hyperglycemia in Seneca Indians" [80] to be high. Diabetes was already diagnosed in 11.5% of men and 14.5% of women in a one-third sample of reservation residents: plasma glucose levels were above 200 mg/100 ml an hour after challenge among 14% of those aged 25 to 34; 12% among 35 to 44 year olds; 15% among 45 to 54 year olds; rising to 33% among those aged 55 to 64 and 39% in the 65 to 74 year old group. Jay H. Stein, et al. found "The High Prevalence of Abnormal Glucose Tolerance in the Cherokee Indians of North Carolina" [185] to be 14% of the 371 volunteers over 34 years of age, using 149 mg/100 ml as the cut-off point. In addition to the 10% already known to have diabetes, this brought the total to 24%.

Among descendants of the old Creek Confederacy, R. C. Elston, et al. in "Studies of Blood and Urine Glucose in Seminole Indians" [86] discovered 3% of studied Florida and 13% of studied Oklahoma Seminoles to have diabetes, at 160.6 mg/100 ml serum glucose mean for the Florida group and 182.6 mg/100 ml mean for the Oklahoma group. The statistically significant difference between these two Seminole populations appears striking in view of their historically recent separation.

Among Yuman-speaking Indians in the Southwest, Robert Earl Henry, et al. found that "Diabetes in the Cocopah Indians" [108] occurred in 17% of 182 persons aged 5 and over, with a 34% incidence among those aged 35 and older.

Northern Piman-speaking peoples are those best studied to date. Max Miller, et al. in "Prevalence of Diabetes mellitus in the American Indians: Results of Glucose Tolerance Tests in the Pima Indians of Arizona" [149] first reported 49% of those aged 30 and over exceeded 160 mg/100 ml. In "Effect of Aging on the Glucose Tolerance Test: Evidence that the Normal Standards Change Only Slightly With Age" Peter H. Bennett, et al. [11] hypothesized that glucose tolerance is distributed among natural populations (such as the Pima) in two components. Bennett, et al. reported that "Diabetes mellitus in American (Pima) Indians" [10] affected a majority of those aged 35 years and over — an "extraordinarily high" prevalence, ten times that of Western Europeans. Norman B. Rushforth, et al. offered further evidence on "Diabetes in the Pima Indians: Evidence of Bimodality in Glucose Tolerance Distributions" [169]. The component with mean glucose levels of 350 mg/100 ml for men and 420 for women reached its maximum size among 36% of the male and 49% for the female Pimas aged 55 to 64. Arthur G. Steinberg, et al. made a "Preliminary Report on the Genetics of Diabetes Among the Pima Indians" [186]. Jeanne M. Reid, et al. analyzed "Nutrient Intake of Pima Indian Women: Relationships to Diabetes mellitus and Gallblader Disease" [165]. They found none: 277 women aged 25 to 44 differed little from women throughout the national population.

Aleš Hrdlička sounded an alarm in *Tuberculosis Among Certain Indian Tribes of the United States* [114]. While he personally studied samples of the Menominee, Oglalá Sioux, Quinaielt, Hupa, and Mojave, Hrdlička's main achievement was eliciting a Bureau of Indian Affairs nation-wide compilation of statistics showing a total tuberculosis case-rate of 26.5 per 1,000 in 1904 and morbidity from the pulmonary type in 1908. Pulmonary tuberculosis affected 9.7 Indians per 1,000 population in 1904; the mortality rate from pulmonary tuberculosis reached 7.9 per 1,000 by 1908, nearly double the rate among Blacks and about 4.6 times that among Whites. When Forrest Clements analyzed "Racial Differences in Mortality and Morbidity" in 1931 [27], tuberculosis was the grim reaper on reservations. He calculated its death rate as 440 per 1,000 among men and 360 among women. He also found a diabetes death rate of 7 per 1,000 among Mojave and Chemehuevi men who died between 1910 and 1930.

In "The World's Oldest On-going Protest: North American Indian Drinking Patterns" Nancy O. Laurie [139] claimed that Indian drinking is no more hazardous to health than karate, mountain climbing, or mushroon hunting. Having known personally two incumbent Tribal Chairmen with high-order abilities, whose combined diabetes and drinking killed them, this author must differ. Moreover, there is some evidence of inherent biological differences in alcohol response. Donald Fenna, et al. in "Ethanol Metabolism in Various Racial Groups" [88] reported that Canadian Indians and Eskimos consistently metabolize alcohol at a rate significantly slower than Canadian Whites. Peter H. Wolff cited Cree Indian facial flushing, pulse pressure, and optical density all greater than among persons of European descent in "Vasomotor Sensitivity to Alcohol in Diverse Mongoloid Populations" [213]. Yet Lurie hypothesized that Indians drink to assert and maintain their Indianness, not because of role conflicts in a multi-ethnic society. She viewed Indian behavioral "alternatives" to drinking as maintaining an exemplary reputation, being an Indian expert or leader. Such behaviors do *not* demonstrably exclude drinking.

Frances N. Ferguson identified "anxiety drinkers" and "recreaction drinkers" in "Navaho Drinking: Some Tentative Hypotheses" [89], drawn from experience in the McKinley County, New Mexico, Community Treatment Plan. Only recreation drinkers responded to treatment which provided them new values in a tribe containing 3,000 estimated alcoholics and 10,000 problem drinkers. Studying "Navajo Suicide" Jerrold E. Levy [136] found nearly half were intoxicated at the time of or just prior to their suicide.

Gerard Littman's "Alcoholism, Illness and Social Pathology among American Indians in Transition" [137] summarizes numerous studies and draws upon experience at St. Augustine's Center for American Indians in Chicago and a study of Mescalero Apaches. In 1968, 23% of adult Mescaleros were problem drinkers (as compared to the 4.5% national incidence), and 44% of reservation deaths were alcohol-related. Littman stressed that individuals differ in intra-familial relationships, tribal background, and degree of transculturation, making difficult the identification of a simple drinking dynamic. Edward P. Dozier advanced a simpler analysis in "Problem Drinking Among American Indians: The Role of Sociocultural Deprivation" [82]. Blaming relative deprivation, Dozier emphasized that group drinking imperatives bring criminal and community disorganizational consequences.

In "Alcohol and the Standing Rock Sioux Tribe, II: Psychodynamics and Cultural Factors in Drinking" James O. Whittaker [208] reported (as did Ferguson and many others) a virtual absence of social sanctions against heavy drinkers or alcoholics. Wesley R. Hurt and Richard M. Brown's "Social Drinking Patterns Among the Yankton Sioux" [116] furnishes ethnographic details on drinking patterns established during the two hundred years of interplay between Sioux cultural mandates and dominant White ones. In "Acculturation Stress and the Functions of Alcohol Among the Forest [County] Potawatomi" John H. Hamer [104] viewed drinking as a means of allowing the individual to escape from anxiety about displaying socially disapproved aggression. Unlike Lurie, Hamer perceived drinking to allow a temporal assumption of a traditional social position interfered with or not substituted for in post-tribal society. Theodore D. Graves's "Acculturation, Access and Alcohol in a Tri-Ethnic Community" [95] finds that Indians drink and become drunk with much greater frequency than Anglo-and Spanish-Americans in the same settlement —

only economically successful, acculturated Indians do not do so.

The historic high incidence of alcohol abuse in Native American populations must be considered a factor in depopulation. David H. Van Thiel, et al. in "Ethanol Inhibition of Vitamin A Metabolism in the Testes: Possible Mechanism for Sterility in Alcoholics" [195] reported that alcohol inhibits spermatogenesis.

There exists no general analysis of colonial warfare's contribution to Native American depopulation. Nonetheless, several investigators have explicitly recognized that warfare significantly depressed Native American population. One first attempt at a regional summary (deficient because it ineorporated Mooney's old figures) was Cook's "Interracial Warfare and Population Decline among the New England Indians" [60]. In three periods of conflict, 1634–35, 1643–45, and 1675–76, Europeans inflicted 1,950 known deaths: perhaps 795 died of wounds; 3,000 of exposure or disease; colonists sold 1,000 as slaves; and 2,000 found refuge with alien tribes — a total loss of 9,745, Cook concluded. In *Primitive Society and Its Vital Statistics* Ludwik Krzywicki [129] expressed the belief that North American tribes engaged in almost incessant warfare. Yet 186 tribes he classed as numbering less than 500 persons; 125 from 500 to 1,000; 120 from 1,000 to 2,500; 44 from 2,500 to 5,000; 21 from 5,000 to 10,000; and 7 over 10,000 were unevenly distributed in different culture areas — an apparent contradiction.

Perhaps the most explicit analysis of the dynamics of lethal historic famine available appears in James L. Ratliff's "What Happened to the Kalapuya? A Study of the Depletion of Their Economic Base" [164]. Aware of epidemic mortality in 1781–82 and 1830–33, Ratliff argued that Métis fur traders starved the Kalapuya to death by seizing their aboriginal trade profits, by farming choice camas-producing plots, by grazing grasshopper-harvesting sites while grist mills preempted prime fishing sites at stream falls. Estimated at 3,000 about 1780, the Kalapuya later became extinct as an ethnic group.

Depopulation Trends

If specific pandemics are poorly documented, their cumulative impacts are somewhat better known, thanks to research into population trends of various Native American peoples in a broad sample of aboriginal culture areas.

Perhaps the most balanced analysis is William E. Unrau's "The Depopulation of the Dheghia–Siouan Kansa Prior to Removal" [207], which explicitly demonstrates how both epidemic and endemic diseases, warfare, natural disasters, malnutrition, and forced migrations all combined to decimate Kansa numbers. John C. Ewers began to analyze "The Influence of Epidemics on the Indian Populations and Cultures of Texas" [87]. He raised to 50,000 Mooney's 42,000 estimate of Texas tribal population prior to 1820 and pointed out their decline to 12,143 by 1890, or less than 25%. Ewers attributed most of this loss to no less than thirty epidemics from 1528 to 1890, as compared to the five Mooney identified. The pre-Columbian population and historic decline were greater: the amalgamation of thirty Caddoan settlements into three indicates nearer a 90% than a 75% depopulation. Ewers drew upon the work of Patrick I. Nixon, who sketched a bare beginning of epidemic and missionized Native American population history in sections of *The Medical Story of Early Texas, 1528–1853* [159].

A noteworthy regional reconstruction of depopulation is Mark F. Boyd, et al., *Here They Once Stood: The Tragic End of the Apalachee Missions* [22]. It describes the destruction of fourteen surviving missions at the beginning of the eighteenth century — a small sample of Florida Indian disappearance under the Spanish colonial mission system and colonial warfare. John T. Lanning's *The Spanish Missions of Georgia* [133] slights population trends but provides some data on numbers. Recent contributions include Kathleen A. Deagan's "*Mestizaje* in Colonial St. Augustine" [74] on ethnic mixture at the military post where surviving Indians were concentrated by 1704; Robert L. Gold's "The Settlement of the Pensacola Indians in New Spain 1763–1770" [92]; and Gold's *Borderland Empires in Transition* [93] on the evacuation of Florida Native Americans and their resettlement near Vera Cruz or in Cuba after the Treaty of 1763.

In "The Significance of Disease in the Extinction of the New England Indians" Cook [61] achieved a first approximation of numerical magnitude in a biological disaster. He attributed 5,550 deaths to an initial 1616–19 plague epidemic and 1,650 to a 1633–34 smallpox epidemic. Cook estimated that endemic diseases diminished groups which escaped the epidemics at a 1.5% per year rate — a rate which leads to rapid group extinction. Wayne C. Temple's *Indian Villages of the Illinois Country* [193] traces migrations and declining populations of ten tribes historically present in Illinois.

In "Indian Diseases as Aids to Pacific Northwest Settlement" Leslie M. Scott [177] noted that Indian armed resistance would have retarded Anglo-American colonization of that area, had Native American numbers not been lowered by 80% or more prior to the Oregon Trail migration. Relying on Mooney's estimates of aboriginal population (and taking into account only two major epidemics) Scott underestimated the extent of depopulation.

Continued interest on the part of University of California scholars largely accounts for the fact that population trends have been more thoroughly analyzed for that state than for any other culture area. Powers, Merriam, and Kroeber have already been mentioned. Cook analyzed in impressive detail many aspects of California Native American population. Labeling mission statistics "far superior to anything else we possess with respect to the North American Indians," Cook reconstructed

Population Trends Among the California Mission Indians [34]. Missionized population rose to 21,000 in 1824, then declined. An initial birthrate of 47 per 1,000 fell 35% due to diminishing numbers of women; a third of the children under age 10 died in an 1806 measles epidemic, and a fourth perished in 1799 and 1828. In "California's First Medical Survey: Report of Surgeon-General José Benites" Cook [30] translated an 1805 report on diseases among neophytes at six missions. Syphilis, tuberculosis, dysentery, pleurisy, inflammatory fevers, and scrofula were in evidence.

In *The Conflict Between the California Indian and White Civilization. I. The Indian Versus the Spanish Mission* Cook [36] summarized mission Indian birth and death rates: the former fell from 45 per 1,000 in 1780 to 32 in 1830; the latter rose from 70 per 1,000 in 1778 to 85 around 1798 before returning to 70 about 1828. Cook reviewed dietary, social, and genetic factors in Native American depopulation, as well as disease, which he calculated caused 45% of the net depopulation.

In the second volume of the same work, *The Physical and Demographic Reaction of the Nonmission Indians in Colonial and Provincial California* Cook [37] estimated the number of Wintun, Maidu, Miwok, Pomo, Wappo, and Yokuts killed in armed conflict with Spaniards and Mexicans as 2,245 to 1848 — 5,000 died from diseases and 4,000 entered missions. In his third volume, *The American Invasion, 1848–1870* Cook [38] estimated that United States armed forces killed 4,000 Native Americans; discounted the effect of "social homicide" on the Indian population; and decided that diseases accounted for fully 60% of the Indian decline. Cook calculated that Anglo-Americans kidnapped 4,000 children for servants within a fifteen-year period beginning with 1852. Economic necessity forced many Indian women into prostitution, further disrupting Native American families and reproduction.

In the fourth and final volume, *Trends in Marriage and Divorce Since 1850* Cook [39] summarized evidence of a historic shift from "Indian custom" to civil marriage under state law, with diminishing integrity of these marital unions.

Spanish colonial records allow reconstruction of the depopulation of the Baja California peninsula. In "Diseases of the Indians of Lower California in the Eighteenth Century" Cook [29] translated a section from an anonymous Jesuit account which mentions epidemics of spotted fever, smallpox, perhaps malaria (1742), and measles (1748), but identifies syphilis as the worst killer. In *The Extent and Significance of Disease among the Indians of Baja California, 1697–1773* Cook [31] underestimated the aboriginal peninsular population at 41,500 — his own density figures imply nearly 55,000 — and outlined its decline to 4,000 in 1773. Cook attributed 25% to 40% of the loss to epidemic diseases — specifically, smallpox in 1709–10 and 1728; typhus and malaria in 1742–44; and measles in 1748 and 1769 — reinforced by endemic syphilis. Aschmann [6] found evidence for epidemic smallpox in 1780–83; measles in 1769 and 1805; unknown diseases in the 1720s, 1755, and 1762–63; and mortality rates (mostly for infants) approaching 100 per 1,000 after 1790, apparently from syphilis. Geographer Peveril Meigs analyzed *The Dominican Mission Frontier of Lower California* [147]. He calculated an aboriginal population density averaging 1.15 persons per mi.^{2} (using a three-mission sample to estimate pre-conversion populations). Meigs discovered that these missions lasted half a century and that diseases introduced into the peninsula caused their decline.

The best cultural history of peoples in the Southwest, Edward H. Spicer's *Cycles of Conquest* [181] places population estimates in environmental and cultural context without primary concern for demography. For the New Mexico Pueblos, Ezra B. W. Zubrow's *Population, Contact, and Climate in the New Mexican Pueblos* [217] fails to correlate historic Pueblo population decline and recovery with climatic variations. Zubrow even failed to attempt a correlation of these trends with Pueblo disease environment, ignoring the pioneering and classic study by Aberle, et al., "The Vital History of San Juan Pueblo" [2]. The latter takes into account not only diseases, but also the other factors mentioned in the above introduction. Dobyns's "Indian Extinction in the Middle Santa Cruz River Valley, Arizona" [77] and *Pioneering Christians Among the Perishing Indians of Tucson* [76] reconstruct the 1700 to 1850 decline among the Northern Piman-speaking population of the San Pedro and Santa

Cruz river valleys. His *Spanish Colonial Tucson: A Demographic History* [79] discusses Northern Piman Indian decline and Mestizo population growth at one multi-ethnic settlement.

Cook and Borah stand out as giants in the analysis of Mesoamerican historic population trends. One can place more faith in the reconstruction of central Mexico's trends than those anywhere else in the New World as a result of their work. In their 1969 "Conquest and Population" summary, Borah and Cook [21] saw total population falling to 16,800,000 in 1532; to 7,300,000 by 1548; to 2,650,000 by 1568; to 1,900,000 in 1585; to 1,275,000 by 1595; and finally, to 1,075,000 by 1605. Had Old World diseases not so decimated Native Americans, Cook and Borah concluded, they would have been able to evict the European interlopers as did the Chinese.

Borah and Cook relied upon a survey of Native American tribute payers (in about half the settlements) for estimating *The Population of Central Mexico in 1548* [18]. Besides secular tribute records, Cook and Borah also utilized sixteenth-century clerical records of total populations or specific segments such as family heads, married men, or confessants, in *The Indian Population of Central Mexico 1531–1610* [63]. The abundant records for 1565–70 enabled them to tabulate a 1568 total of 2,650,000, or a range between 2,500,000 and 2,800,000. By calculating ratios from town samples reported at other times, they estimated the 1532, 1580, 1595, and 1605 figures given above. Their regional analysis indicates annual depopulation rates of 3.74% in the highlands and 6.87% in the lowlands from 1532 to 1570. In some of these analyses and especially in "On the Credibility of Contemporary Testimony on the Population of Mexico in the Sixteenth Century" Cook and Borah [64] tested the accuracy of their techniques for estimating Native American populations from fiscal and missionary records. They found sixty settlements with such data — Indian residents having stated pre-Conquest population size when interviewed by royal representatives after a 1577 order. They calculated that the Indian statements averaged only 8.6% lower than their "depletion index" estimates. Significantly, Cook and Borah came within 3.8% of the Indian figures for the "intermediate altitude" zone from which their settlement sample of twenty-seven is the largest. They varied by 38.5% from Indian figures for fifteen plateau settlements and by 31% from eighteen coastal places. Borah's "Population Decline and the Social and Institutional Changes of New Spain in the Middle Decades of the Sixteenth Century" [14] documents that depopulation generated Spanish colonial reforms. These changes benefited Native American serfs and slaves, and virtually abolished the native nobility, greatly simplifying the structure of Indian society. In *New Spain's Century of Depression* Borah [13] stressed that Native American population decline resulted in a century-long economic depression. Growing Spanish and Mestizo urban populations paid dearly for food and fuel during the seventeenth century.

Cook and Borah's *The Population of the Mixteca Alta 1520–1960* [65] calculates some 600,000 to 800,000 inhabitants prior to Conquest — a density producing serious erosion, even with digging-stick cultivation. In this pioneer study of regional population decline and recovery, they concluded that the total fell to 528,000 by 1531, then 100,000 in 1568, and only 57,000 by 1590. In the 1660–70 decade it was about 30,000. Population increased to 54,000 in 1742, to 73,922 in 1777, and to 76,000 in 1803. The wars of independence lowered the figures to 64,549 in 1826, and they there upon rose to 133,483 in 1878, to 180,584 in 1910, and to 261,177 by 1960.

For Mexico's smallest state, Robert A. Halberstein, et al. perform a "Historical–Demographic Analysis of Indian population in Tlaxcala, Mexico" [103]. From colonial census data, they traced a decline from 300,000 in 1519 to 250,000 in 1531, to 196,703 in 1556, to 150,000 in 1575, and to about 100,000 by 1600 — largely the result of epidemic diseases. Cook's *Santa Maria Ixcatlán: Habitat, Population, Subsistence* [53] focuses mainly on man–environment relationships, but sketches Ixcateco population trends. From 10,000 prior to Spanish sovereignty, this group dropped to about 500 by 1610; rose to 886 in 1895; peaked at 1,113 in 1945; and dropped thereafter through emigration.

Population Recovery

Native American numbers began to recover after

crucial improvements occurred in smallpox prevention, as summarized by the Stearns [184]. Cook described Spanish colonial efforts to introduce smallpox vaccination to New Spain in 1804–1805 in "Francisco Xavier Balmis and the Introduction of Vaccination to Latin America" [35]. Cook skeptically analyzed James Ohio Pattie's retrospective account of vaccinating many Californians in 1828 in "Smallpox in Spanish and Mexican California, 1770–1845" [32]. Cook presented mortality figures for 1823–28 at seven missions showing continued population decline, and summarized the "Miramontes" epidemic in 1838–39, which had killed from 60,000 to 300,000 tribesmen according to the suppositions of witnesses.

Reporting *Physiological and Medical Observations Among the Indians of Southwestern United States and Northern Mexico,* Aleš Hrdlička [113] compiled evidence of late nineteenth-century population recovery. San Carlos Apache and Pima women past the normal age of childbearing averaged seven births; 40% of the former and 33% of the latter offspring survived, an approximate 39% Apache and 19% Pima rate of increase per generation.

Wilton M. Krogman in 1935 reported "Vital Data on the Population of the Seminole Indians of Florida and Oklahoma" [128] and stressed the importance of over 55% of the population being 19 years old or younger — clearly a growing population. Clark Wissler's 1936 analysis of "Distribution of Death Among American Indians" [211] documents a Pine Ridge Sioux reservation community birth rate of 42 per 1,000 and a death rate of 37 per 1,000 in 1916–29, during a period of growth. Wissler compared Dakota trends to those of other reservation residents in *Changes in Population Profiles Among the Northern Plains Indians* [210]. In *Population Changes Among the Northern Plains Indians* Wissler [212] compiled United States and Canadian statistics showing tribal reservation population nadirs followed by recovery: about 1894 for United States Piegan; 1909 for Gros Ventre and Western Cree; 1914 for Blood; 1924 for Canadian Piegan and United States Blackfeet; while the Sarsi declined until 1929.

The classic analysis of population recovery among a Native American group remains the San Juan study by Aberle, et al. [2], showing an average 1.5% increase per year after 1910. Aberle used mission records and interviews with San Juan and Santa Clara women to discover that "Frequency of Pregnancies and Birth Intervals Among Pueblo Indians" [1] had been stable since 1800; after 1863, population increased 0.5% per year until 1890. Stephen J. Kunitz in "Factors Influencing Recent Navajo and Hopi Population Changes" [131] found that Hopi recovery began about 1900; accelerated as post-1930s sanitation and health care improvements lowered the death rate; and slowed in the 1960s after the birth rate fell to 25 per 1,000, while the Navajo birth and growth rates remained high.

The most precise recording of representative sample

subpopulation of Navajos by Walsh McDermott, et al. during a "Health Care Experiment at Many Farms" [141] finds annual growth to be an extraordinary 4%, with an average birth rate of 45.8 and death rate of 6.2 per 1,000. Kunitz calculated "Navajo and Hopi Fertility 1971–1972" [132] as 28 to 34 per 1,000 for Navajos, 19 to 21 for reservation and 28 to 36 per 1,000 for non-reservation Hopis.

Norbert Hirschorn and Gary H. Spivey assessed "Health and the White Mountain Apache" [111], finding an average annual increase of "an astonishing " 3.8% per year in 1965–71, despite 76 deaths per 1,000 live births during the first year.

In his 1957 "Demography of the American Indians," J. Nixon Hadley [102] projected (from the 70% increase in the period 1900 to 1950) a 50% increase to 720,000 U. S. Indians in 1975. In fact, that figure was exceeded by 1970. Recovery therefore, proceeds far faster than had been expected. Many cases are representative of the post–World War II trends. Charles A. Bishop discovered, for example, and reported in *The Northern Ojibwa and the Fur Trade* [12] that one Canadian band doubled in population between 1946 and 1970, and had quadrupled in a century.

Under the stereotypic title "The Vanishing Indian," the physical anthropologist Aleš Hrdlička [115] noted in 1917 that enumerated Indians were mostly of mixed ancestry, and full-bloods nearly extinct. Yet, the process of intergroup mixture receives more social recognition in many parts of Latin America than North America. C. E. Marshall's 1939 "The Birth of the Mestizo in New Spain" [144] emphasizes royal encouragement of intermarriage by land grant, emigration and welfare policies, and Indian women's motivations to bear Mestizo children not subject to tribute. These factors created a group comprising 6% of the non-Indian population by 1560 or so, and a majority before 1930. In their 1971 *Essays* Cook and Borah [66] analyzed Mexican inter-ethnic mixture in some detail.

In various works, Cook and Borah identified colonial factors such as debt peonage, Native American migration to Spanish towns, and ethnic interbreeding as slowing Native American population recovery and making contemporary Mexico a stronghold of the "New American Race." Borah included these matters in *New Spain's Century of Depression* [13]. Borah and Cook also mentioned them in *The Population of Central Mexico in 1548* [18]. Cook analyzed "Migration as a Factor in the History of Mexican Population: Sample Data from West Central Mexico, 1743–1950" [59]. Consulting censuses and civil records, Cook found the number of migrants inversely related to the distance they moved; a steady transfer into middle west coast areas, slowing in this century; and an increase in the distance moved in recent decades, accompanied by accelerating rural migration to Guadalajara.

D. A. Brading and Celia Wu traced ethnic mixture in one *municipio* (country-like area) in "Population Growth and Crisis: Leon, 1720–1860" [23]. The 1742 population of 16,970 increased to 172,432 in 1882. Two late eighteenth-century samples show a quarter of the Spaniards marrying Mestizos or Mulattos; a third of the Mulattos marrying Spaniards, Mestizos, or Indians; and the Indians marrying into other groups as they coalesced with the Mulattos. At the national level, Moisés González Navarro, "*Mestizaje* in Mexico During the National Period" [94] provides a fine summation.

In Canada and the United States many so-called Native Americans actually possess more European than New World forebears. Hypocritical English-speaking society tends to define a person with any Indian genes as a "Native American," a social process parallel to that which regards a person with any African genes as an Afro-American. Cook pioneered analysis of the creation of a "New American Race" in his "Racial Fusion among the California and Nevada Indians" [41], finding a tendency for "mixed-bloods" to marry Whites, leaving behind a steadily diminishing pool of "full-bloods." Reservations did, however, impose some barriers to mixing. In "Migration and Urbanization of the Indians in California" Cook [40] discovered a tendency for "Indian" women to migrate to cities and marry non-Indians long before 1928, when 13% of the state's "Indians" had migrated.

Cook's "Demographic Consequences of European Contact With Primitive Peoples" [42] observes that miscegenation produced a Euro-American "new human variety," but concludes that North American tribesmen were "rapidly approaching total amalgamation" into a more numerous White population. William H. Gilbert in "Surviving Indian Groups of the Eastern United States" [90] noted that these ethnic groups included (by 1948) very low proportions of even putative "full-bloods," as for example Rhode Island's 19.5%. A most explicit analysis of the creation of one segment of the "New American Race" under a tribal label appears in Unrau's fine Kansa paper [207].

Definition of the "New American Race" under old tribal labels is not only a social but also a legal process vital to some individuals entitled by acts of Congress to "per capita" payouts of cash benefits from mineral royalties or court awards, and to free medical services, house lots, farms, and ranches not subject to state or local real estate taxes. Hence it is easy to understand what prompted Sylvester Tinker's *Authentic Osage Indian Roll Book* [197]. Because few such rolls have been published, demographic analysis of such data lies in the future.

Demographic Case Studies

Recent serious demographic analysis of post-tribal Native Americans has been published for the most part in the form of specific ethnic group case studies.

The phenomenal growth of today's largest single Native American ethnic group, the Navajos, has already been mentioned. The most ambitious attempt to analyze Navajo population trends since 1848 is *An Analysis of*

Sources of Information on the Population of the Navajo by Denis F. Johnston [121]. It is a compilation rather than an analysis. William Kelly's *Methods and Resources for the Construction and Maintenance of Navajo Population Register* [124] suggests the means for arriving at an accurate enumeration of Navajos without venturing into estimates. R. Chris Brown, et al. assessed "The Epidemiology of Accidents Among the Navajo Indians" [24]. Accidents are the major cause of death, and automobile–pedestrian accidents represent the largest single type of such fatalities.

The most intensively studied post-tribal North American population in recent years has been the Northern Piman-speakers. The United States Public Health Service, aided by research contractors, set out to establish an accurate total register for the "Papago" reservation-dwelling portion of that group in order to accumulate medical records for swift location and analysis as aid in diagnosis and treatment.

J. W. Hoover's "Generic Descent of the Papago Villages" [112] pioneered in 1935 by the reconstruction of post-1860 land colonization from oral accounts. Later analysts more or less follow Hoover, but often extrapolate his data to earlier time periods without justification. In *Papagos in the Cotton Fields, 1950* Dobyns [75] provided approximate numbers for those residing and seasonally laboring off-reservation. Bertram L. Hanna, et al., "A Preliminary Study of the Population of the Pima Indians" [105] argues from blood group antigen distributions among 97 often-related individuals to conclusions — highly dubious in part — about the prehistoric origin of the Gila River Pimas. The antigens indicate a 6% to 7% historic European admixture.

Then, long-range systematic study of the "Papago" subpopulation began. Robert A. Hackenberg's *Papago Population Study* [97] and William H. Kelly's *The Papago Indians of Arizona* [123] laid the groundwork for a population register. Delmos J. Jones's "A Description of Settlement Pattern and Population Movement on the Papago Reservation" [122] points out that these desert dwellers no longer move as transhumant village units. Families move in many different directions: permanent villages, farms, ranches, homesteads, and to long-term employment off-reservation. Hackenberg in "An Anthropological Study of Demographic Transition: The Papago Information System" [98] set forth the general goals for creation of a "demographic information system" for Papagos. He stressed how improvement of health services by using such a system depends upon accurate correlation of information about individuals and medical treatments despite the changing of names and migration. Hackenberg described "The Parameters of an Ethnic Group: A Method for Studying the Total Tribe" [99] using aerial photographs and electronic data-processing for socio-medical data obtained by interview. Conventional records account for only three-fourths of the individuals so identified. Hackenberg claimed Papago numbers doubled in this century; therefore population and society were no longer congruent by 1967.

This massive effort to compile patient case histories and pedigrees had generated numerous partial population analyses without overt concern for the invasion of individual privacy. Jerry D. Niswander, et al. in "Population Studies on Southwestern Indian Tribes. I. History, Culture, and Genetics of the Papago" [158] abstracted reports of blood antigen analysts whose conclusions, however dressed up by statistical manipulation, are largely vitiated by their reliance upon secondary and often quite speculative historical sources and their miscomprehension of those consulted. Peter L. Workman and Jerry D. Niswander in "Population Studies on Southwestern Indian Tribes. II. Local Genetic Differentiation in the Papago" [216] concluded that ten grazing–political districts contain ten subpopulations with considerable endogamy and ancestral influence on contemporary genotype. They failed to recognize actual historic tribes that account for the founder effect, or known migrations that strongly influence intergroup similarities and differences. From population register data reported in "Modernization, Population, Dispersion and Papago Genetic Integrity" David G. Smith [180] showed that nearly half the sample Papagos born prior to 1900 married outside their villages of origin, and nearly half of the latter traveled outside the district for a mate. Village and district exogamy has been increasing ever since. His analysis invalidates the Workman–

Niswander assumption of district endogamy.

In "Epidemiological Studies of Papago Indian Mortality" Herman A. Tyroler and Ralph Patrick [200] utilized the register to determine an annual crude death-rate of 8.8 per 1,000, with 9.8 among males and 7.9 among females. They distinguished a markedly higher birth rate among Papagos in "modern" settlements than traditional ones to account for most of a 2.8% annual rate of increase. Julie M. Uhlmann analyzed "The Impact of Modernization on Papago Indian Fertility" [202], finding that women in Tucson differ from all other Papago women in bearing both the first and last child at a younger age. They therefore constitute "the leading edge of change" in fertility bahavior. Just as Michael S. Teitelbaum questioned the "Relevance of Demographic Transition Theory for Developing Countries" [192], one may likewise question its relevance for the Northern Piman-speaking Indians.

Robert A. Hackenberg and C. Roderick Wilson considered "Reluctant Emigrants: The Role of Migration in Papago Indian Adaptation" [101] in terms of a sample of the register from three demonstrably unrepresentative districts. They reported that a third of those reared in reservation villages emigrate outside it, women leaving more frequently than men, so that 18% of reservation males cannot find Papago wives. Consequently, the population remaining in reservation settlements increases at 1.4% annually and will not double for half a century. Hackenberg and Mary M. Gallagher considered

"The Costs of Cultural Change: Accidental Injury and Modernization among the Papago Indians" [100] by region on the reservation. The region with their highest modernization score has an accident report rate double that of the more traditional regions. In a more sophisticated analysis, Donald D. Stull in "Victims of Modernization: Accident Rates and Papago Indian Adjustment" [188] determined that "modern" individuals suffer significantly more accidents than "traditional" persons in both modern and traditional villages. Thus, "modern" individuals living in "modern" villages suffer much the highest accident rate.

Infectious diseases, particularly diarrheas and pneumonia, most often endanger Papago infants, according to Morton S. Adams, et al., who analyzed "Health of Papago Indian Children" [3].

For the ranchería-dwelling Indians, Moni Nag spent a month collecting data on age of women at menarche, age at marriage, maternity ratio, pregnancy ratio, child–woman ratio, etc. among Walapais and Havasupais. His findings are reported in *Factors Affecting Human Fertility in Nonindustrial Societies: A Cross Cultural Study* [155]. Employing similar reasoning, Anita L. Alvarado hypothesized "Cultural Determinants of Population Stability in the Havasupai Indians" [4]. In fact, Havasupai numbers declined in the period from 1776 to 1906, and then increased. Inasmuch as Alvarado's cultural factors remained constant, they are irrelevant to actual trends.

For Sonoran desert and peninsular California peoples, Herbert R. Harvey's "Population of the Cahuilla Indians: Decline and Its Causes" [106] provides an illustrative analysis. Combining mid-nineteenth-century reports by military officers with recent ethnographic research, Harvey placed early 1850s population at 2,500, with a 46% reduction by 1890 to 1,539 or so.

Martin I. Glassner compiled "Population Figures for Mandan Indians" [91] on the Great Plains. He provided minimal interpretation of estimates from La Verendrye's 15,000 in 1738 to the present (other than to comment that probably none is accurate); nor did he interpret several maps of village locations he reproduced.

Enumerations

The sorry state of colonial knowledge of Native American numbers is summed up by Evarts B. Greene and Virginia D. Harrington's *American Population Before the Federal Census of 1790* [96] in 54 guesses and estimates dating from 1677 to 1789. Since independence, at least four federal departments have on occasion enumerated Native Americans — War, Interior, Commerce, and Health, Education and Welfare.

The quantitative orientation of military leaders has generated estimates and counts of tribesmen. In *A Report to the Secretary of War of the United States on Indian Affairs* Jedidiah Morse [153] included a table of tribal populations totaling 471,136 in a nation still suffering its growing pains. An example of a later local enumeration is that of San Carlos Reservation residents by surgeon Frederick Lloyd, *San Carlos Agency, Arizona* [138] in 1883. He distinguished some tribes and lumped together others. He differentiated adults from children by sex, as in the case of 313 Western Yavapais: 131 men, 99 women, 49 boys, and 34 girls.

As authorized by Congress, Henry R. Schoolcraft embarked the new Bureau of Indian Affairs on the enumeration of Indians and reported the results in his massive *Information Respecting the History, Condition and Prospects of the Indian Tribes of the United States* [176]. He reported government agents in contact with 313,264 Indians in 1857. Later, the *Annual Reports* of the Commissioners of Indian Affairs to the Secretaries of the Interior for many years included relatively accurate to grossly erroneous estimates of reservation or tribal populations. The local agents reporting Northern Piman numbers, for example, usually guessed. Agents often simply repeated their own or their predecessors' estimates or counts year after year; it is doubtful that such statistics bore a very close relationship to actual trends. Some agents, however, did conscientiously enumerate people. The seriously distorted sex ratio of Mescalero Apaches at the end of their long struggle against European domination, the continued decline in numbers caused by the shortage of childbearing women, and the psychological and biological shocks of adjusting to a restricted reservation land base are all quite apparent in the agents' reports. Later agents recorded reinforcement by migration, the balancing of the sex ratio, and the commencement of the recovery (well into this century) of population growth.

Every decade, the United States Bureau of the Census attempts to enumerate Native Americans along with the general population. Native Americans generally maintain that census takers do a poor job of it. Anthropologists who study these matters agree. Part of their low opinion stems, however, from differences in definitions. Census enumerators lack the time required to record as an Indian every person legally defined by the Bureau of Indian Affairs as such. The census depends upon self-identification. Consequently, it reports many individuals who claim to be Native Americans (such as the Lumbees in North Carolina) but are not legally so defined; it omits many individuals (such as some reservation-dwelling Navajos) who are legally Indians. Thus, national census reports must be consulted with caution. They provide, nonetheless, some kinds of demographic information about Native Americans available nowhere else.

The first census report specifically valuable for Native American demography is that of 1890. Census officials made a special effort to count Native Americans with accuracy during this census, resulting in a *Report of Indians Taxed and Indians Not Taxed in the United States* [203]. The enumerated Native American population increased from 248,253 in 1890 to 265,683 in 1910 — a 7% rise heralded as the beginning of population recovery

[99] 1967. "The Parameters of an Ethnic Group: A Method for Studying the Total Tribe." *American Anthropologist* 69:478–92.

[100] Hackenberg, Robert Allan and Gallagher, Mary M. 1972. "The Costs of Cultural Change: Accidental Injury and Modernization among the Papago Indians." *Human Organization* 31:211–26.

[101] Hackenberg, Robert Allan and Wilson, C. Roderick. 1972. "Reluctant Emigrants: The Role of Migration in Papago Indian Adaptation." *Human Organization* 31:171–86.

[102] Hadley, J. Nixon. 1957. "Demography of the American Indians." *Annals of the American Academy of Political and Social Sciences* 311:23–30.

[103] Halberstein, Robert A.; Crawford, Michael H.; and Nutini, Hugo G. 1973. "Historical–Demographic Analysis of Indian Populations in Tlaxcala, Mexico." *Social Biology* 20:40–50.

[104] Hamer, John H. 1965. "Acculturation Stress and the Functions of Alcohol Among the Forest [County] Potawatomi." *Quarterly Journal of Studies on Alcohol* 26:285–303.

[105] Hanna, Bertram L.; Dahlberg, Albert A.; and Standskov, Herluf H. 1953. "A Preliminary Study of the Population History of the Pima

Indians." *American Journal of Human Genetics* 5:377–88.

[106] Harvey, Herbert R. 1967. "Population of the Cahuilla Indians: Decline and Its Causes." *Eugenics Quarterly* 14:185–98.

[107] Heizer, Robert Fleming. 1960. "Agriculture and the Theocratic State in Lowland Southeastern Mexico." *American Antiquity* 26:215–22.

[108] Henry, Robert Earl; Burch, Thomas A.; Bennett, Peter H.; and Miller, Max. 1969. "Diabetes in the Cocopah Indians." *Diabetes* 18:33–37.

[109] Hester, Joseph A., Jr. 1953. "Agriculture, Economy and Population Densities of the Maya." In *Carnegie Institution of Washington Yearbook,* vol. 51, pp. 266–70 and vol. 52, pp. 288–92. Washington, D.C.: Carnegie Institution of Washington.

[110] Hillery, George A., Jr. and Essene, Frank J. 1963. "Navajo Population: An Analysis of the 1960 Census." *Southwestern Journal of Anthropology* 19:297–313.

[111] Hirschhorn, Norbert and Spivey, Gary H. 1972. "Health and the White Mountain Apache." [Editorial] *Journal of Infectious Diseases* 126:348–50.

[112] Hoover, J. W. 1935. "Generic Descent of the

Papago Villages." *American Anthropologist* 37:257-64.

Hrdlička, Aleš (Alois Ferdinand).

[113] 1908. *Physiological and Medical Observations Among the Indians of Southwestern United States and Northern Mexico.* Smithsonian Institution. Bureau of American Ethnology, Bulletin:34. Washington, D.C.: Government Printing Office.

[114] 1909. *Tuberculosis Among Certain Indian Tribes of the United States.* Smithsonian Institution, Bureau of American Ethnology, Bulletin:42. Washington, D.C.: Government Printing Office.

[115] 1917. "The Vanishing Indian." *Science* 46:266-67.

[116] Hurt, Wesley R. and Brown, Richard M. 1965. "Social Drinking Patterns of the Yankton Sioux." *Human Organization* 24:222-30.

Jacobs, Wilbur R.

*[117] 1971. "The Fatal Confrontation: Early Native-White Relations on the Frontiers of Australia, New Guinea, and America—A Comparative Study." *Pacific Historical Review* 40:283-309.

[118] 1974. "The Tip of an Iceberg: Pre-Columbian

Indian Demography and Some Implications for Revisionism." *William and Mary Quarterly* (3d ser.) 31:123-32.

[119] Jarcho, Saul 1964. "Some Observations on Diseases in Prehistoric America." *Bulletin of the History of Medicine* 38:1-19.

[120] Jenness, Diamond. 1934. *The Indians of Canada.* 2nd ed. National Museum of Canada, Bulletin: 65, Anthropological Series:15. Ottawa: Department of Mines.

[121] Johnston, Denis Foster. 1966. *An Analysis of Sources of Information on the Population of the Navaho.* Smithsonian Institution, Bureau of American Ethnology, Bulletin: 197. Washington, D. C.: U. S. Government Printing Office.

[122] Jones, Delmos J. 1962. "A Description of Settlement Pattern and Population Movement on the Papago Reservation." *The Kiva* (Apr.) 27:1-9.

Kelly, William Henderson.

[123] 1963. *The Pagago Indians of Arizona: A Population and Economic Study.* Tucson: University of Arizona, Bureau of Ethnic Research, Department of Anthropology.

[124] 1964. *Methods and Resources for the Construction*

and Maintenance of a Navajo Population Register. Tucson: University of Arizona, Bureau of Ethnic Research, Department of Anthropology.

Kroeber, Alfred Louis.

[125] 1925. *Handbook of The Indians of California.* Smithsonian Institution, Bureau of American Ethnology, Bulletin: 78. Washington, D.C.: Government Printing Office.

[126] 1934. "Native American Population." *American Anthropologist* 36:1–25.

[127] 1939. *Cultural and Natural Areas of Native North America.* University of California Publications in American Archaeology and Ethnology:38. Berkeley: University of California Press.

[128] Krogman, Wilton Marion. 1935. "Vital Data on the Population of the Seminole Indians of Florida and Oklahoma." *Human Biology* 7:335–49.

[129] Krzywicki, Ludwik. 1934. *Primitive Society and Its Vital Statistics,* trans. Eleanor Kennedy and Adam Truszkowski. London: Macmillan and Co., Ltd.

[130] Kubler, George. 1942. "Population Movements in Mexico, 1520–1600." *Hispanic American Historical Review* 22:606–43.

Kunitz, Stephen J.
[131] 1974. "Factors Influencing Recent Navajo and Hopi Population Changes." *Human Organization* 33:7–16.
[132] 1974. "Navajo and Hopi Fertility, 1971–1972." *Human Biology* 46:435–51.
[133] Lanning, John Tate. 1935. *The Spanish Missions of Georgia*. Chapel Hill: University of North Carolina Press.
[134] Lasersohn, William. 1965. "Acute Diarrheal Diseases in a Zuñi Community." *Public Health Reports* 80:457–61.
[135] Leikind, Morris E. 1940. "Colonial Epidemic Diseases." *Ciba Symposia* 1:372–78.
[136] Levy, Jerrold E. 1965. "Navajo Suicide." *Human Organization* 24:308–18.
[137] Littman, Gerard. 1970. "Alcoholism, Illness and Social Pathology among American Indians in Transition." *American Journal of Public Health and the Nation's Health* 60:176–87.
[138] Lloyd, Frederick. 1883. *Special Report on Indians at San Carlos Agency, Arizona*. n.p.
[139] Lurie, Nancy Oestriech. 1971. "The World's Oldest On-going Protest: North American Indian Drinking Patterns." *Pacific Historical Review* 40:311–32.

[140] McBryde, F. Webster. 1940. "Influenza in America During the Sixteenth Century (Guatemala: 1523, 1559–1562, 1576)." *Bulletin of the History of Medicine* 8:296–302.

[141] McDermott, Walsh,; Deuschle, Kurt W.; and Barnett, Clifford R. 1972. "Health Care Experiment at Many Farms." *Science* 175:23–31.

[142] MacLeod, William Christie. 1928. *The American Indian Frontier.* New York: A. A. Knopf.

[143] MacNeish, Richard S. 1970. "Social Implications of Changes in Population and Settlement Pattern of the 12,000 Years of Prehistory in the Tehuacan Valley of Mexico." In *Population and Economics,* ed. Paul Deprez, pp. 215–50. See [17].

[144] Marshall, C. E. 1939. "The Birth of the Mestizo in New Spain." *Hispanic American Historical Review* 19:161–84.

[145] Martin, Calvin. 1976. "Wildlife Diseases as a Factor in the Depopulation of the North American Indian." *The Western Historical Quarterly* 7:47–62.

[146] Martin, Paul S. 1973. "The Discovery of America." *Science* 179:969–74.

[147] Meigs, Peveril, 3d. 1935. *The Dominican Mission Frontier of Lower California.* University of

California Publications in Geography:7. Berkeley: University of California Press.

[148] Merriam, Clinton Hart. 1905. "The Indian Population of California." *American Anthropologist* 7:594–606.

[149] Miller, Max; Burch, Thomas A.; Bennett, Peter H.; and Steinberg, Arthur G. 1965. "Prevalence of Diabetes mellitus in the American Indians: Results of Glucose Tolerance Tests in the Pima Indians of Arizona." [Abstract] *Diabetes* 14:439–40.

Mooney, James.

[150] 1910. "Population." In *Handbook of the American Indians North of Mexico*, ed. Frederick Webb Hodge, Smithsonian Institution, Bureau of American Ethnology Bulletin:30, 2 vols., vol. 2, pp. 286–87. Washington, D.C.: Government Printing Office.

[151] 1928. *The Aboriginal Population of America North of Mexico*. Smithsonian Institution, Miscellaneous Collection:80, no. 7. Washington, D.C.: Smithsonian Institution.

[152] Morley, Sylvanus Griswold. 1956. *The Ancient Maya*. 3d ed., rev. by George W. Brainerd. Stanford, Calif.: Stanford University Press.

[153] Morse, Jedidiah. 1822. *A Report to the Secretary of*

War of the United States, on Indian Affairs, Comprising a Narrative of a Tour Performed in the Summer of 1820, Under a Commission from the President of the United States, for the Purpose of Ascertaining, for the Use of the Government, the Actual State of the Indian Tribes in Our Country. New Haven: S. Converse. (Reprinted, New York: Augustus M. Kelley, 1970.)

[154] Mouratoff, George J.; Carroll, Nicholas V.; and Scott, Edward M. 1969. "Diabetes mellitus in Athabaskan Indians in Alaska." *Diabetes* 18:29–32.

[155] Nag, Moni. 1962. *Factors Affecting Human Fertility in Nonindustrial Societies; A Cross-Cultural Study.* Yale University Publications in Anthropology:66. New Haven: Department of Anthropology, Yale University.

[156] Naroll, Raoul. 1962. "Floor Area and Settlement Population." *American Antiquity* 27:587–89.

[157] Neel, James V. 1962. "Diabetes mellitus: a 'Thrifty' Genotype Rendered Detrimental by 'Progress'?" *American Journal of Human Genetics* 14:353–62.

[158] Niswander, Jerry D.; Brown, Kenneth S.; Iba, Barbara Y.; Leyshon, W. C.; and Workman,

Peter L. 1970. "Population Studies on Southwestern Indian Tribes. I. History, Culture, and Genetics of the Papago." *American Journal of Human Genetics* 22:7–23.

[159] Nixon, Patrick Ireland. 1946. *The Medical Story of Early Texas, 1528–1853*. Lancaster, Pa.: Mollie Bennett Lupe Memorial Fund.

[160] Packard, Francis R. 1931. *History of Medicine in the United States*. New York: Paul B. Hoeber, Inc. (Reprinted, New York: Hafner Pub. Co., 1963.)

Powers, Stephen.

[161] 1872. "The Northern California Indians, N° V." *Overland Monthly* 9:305–313.

[162] 1875. "California Indian Characteristics." *Overland Monthly* 14:297–309. (Reprinted as "Tribes of California" in *Contributions of North American Ethnology*, 8 vols. in 9, vol. 3. (1890), ed. John Wesley Powell. U. S. Geographical and Geological Survey of the Rocky Mountain Region. Washington, D.C.: Government Printing Office, 1877–93 [after 1879 published under the supervision of the Bureau of American Ethnology].)

[163] Quaife, Milo M., ed. 1930. "The Smallpox Epidemic on the Upper Missouri." *Mississippi Valley Historical Review* 17:278–99

[164] Ratcliff, James L. 1973. "What Happened to the

Kalapuya? A Study of the Depletion of Their Economic Base." *The Indian Historian* (Summer) 6:27–33.

[165] Reid, Jeanne M.; Fullmer, Sandra D.; Pettigrew, Karen D.; Burch, Thomas A.; Bennett, Peter H.; Miller, Max; and Whedon, G. Donald. 1971. "Nutrient Intake of Pima Indian Women: Relationships to Diabetes mellitus and Gallblader Disease." *American Journal of Clinical Nutrition* 24:1281–89.

[166] Ricketson, Oliver Garrison, Jr. and Ricketson, Edith Bayles. 1937. *Uaxactun, Guatemala. Group E—1926–1931.* Carnegie Institution of Washington, Publication:477. Washington, D.C.: Carnegie Institution of Washington.

[167] Romaniuk, Anatol and Piché, Victor L. 1972. "Natality Estimates for the Canadian Indians by Stable Population Models, 1900–1969." *Canadian Review of Sociology and Anthropology* 9:1–20.

[168] Rubenstein, Alfred; Boyle, Joseph; Odoroff, Charles L.; and Kunitz, Stephen J. 1969. "Effect of Improved Sanitary Facilities on Infant Diarrhea in a Hopi Village." *Public Health Reports* 84:1093–97.

[169] Rushforth, Norman B.; Bennett, Peter H.; Steinberg, Arthur G.; Burch, Thomas A.; and

Miller, Max. 1971. "Diabetes in the Pima Indians. Evidence of Bimodality in Glucose Tolerance Distributions." *Diabetes* 20:756–65.

*[170] Sánchez-Albornoz, Nicolás. 1974. *The Population of Latin America; A History*, trans. W. A. R. Richardson. Berkeley: University of California Press.

Sanders, William T.

[171] 1953. "The Anthropogeography of Central Veracruz." *Revista Mexicana de Estudios Antropológicos* [*Huastecos, Totonacos y sus Vecinos*] 13:27–78.

[172] 1972. "Population, Agricultural History, and Societal Evolution in Mesoamerica." In *Population Growth: Anthropological Implications*, ed. Brian Spooner, pp. 101–53. Cambridge, Mass.: M. I. T. Press.

Sauer, Carl Ortwin.

[173] 1935. *Aboriginal Population of Northwestern Mexico*. Ibero-Americana:10. Berkeley: University of California Press.

[174] 1948. *Colima of New Spain in the Sixteenth Century*. Ibero-Americana:29. Berkeley: University of California Press.

[175] 1966. *The Early Spanish Main*. Berkeley: University of California Press.

[176] Schoolcraft, Henry Rowe. 1851–57. *Historical and Statistical Information Respecting the History, Condition and Prospects of the Indian Tribes of the United States, collected and prepared under the direction of the Bureau of Indian Affairs, per Act of Congress of March 3d, 1847.* Illustrated S. Estman, 6 vols. Philadelphia: Lippincott, Grambo and Co. [Reprinted and reissued numerous times under various titles, all of which contain substantially similiar information.]

[177] Scott, Leslie M. 1928. "Indian Diseases as Aids to Pacific Northwest Settlement." *Oregon Historical Quarterly* 29:144–61.

[178] Shattuck, George Cheever, et al. 1933. *The Peninsula of Yucatan; Medical, Biological, Meteorological and Sociological Studies.* Carnegie Institution of Washington, Publication:431. Washington, D. C.; Carnegie Institution of Washington.

[179] Simmons, Marc. 1966. "New Mexico's Smallpox Epidemic of 1780–1781." *New Mexico Historical Review* 41:319–26.

[180] Smith, David G. 1972. "Modernization, Population, Dispersion, and Papago Genetic Integrity." *Human Organization* 31:187–99.

[181] Spicer, Edward Holland. 1962. *Cycles of Conquest; The Impact of Spain, Mexico, and the United*

States on the Indians of the Southwest, 1533–1960. Tucson: University of Arizona Press.

[182] Spinden, Herbert J. 1928. "The Population of Ancient America." *The Geographical Review* 18:641–60.

[183] Stage, H. H. and Gjullin, C. M. 1935. "Anopheles and Malaria in the Pacific Northwest." *Northwest Science* 9:5–11.

[184] Stearn, Esther Angelica and Stearn, Allen E. 1945. *The Effect of Smallpox on the Destiny of the Amerindian.* Boston: Bruce Humphries, Inc.

[185] Stein, Jay H.; West, Kelly M.; Robey, James M.; Tirador, Dean F.; and McDonald, Glenn W. 1965. "The High Prevalence of Abnormal Glucose Tolerance in the Cherokee Indians of North Carolina." *Archives of Internal Medicine* 116:842–45.

[186] Steinberg, Arthur G.; Rushforth, Norman B.; Bennett, Peter H.; Burch, Thomas A; and Miller, Max. 1970. "Preliminary Report on the Genetics of Diabetes Among the Pima Indians." *Advanced Metabolic Disorders* (Supplement) 1:11–21.

*[187] Stewart, Thomas Dale. 1973. *The People of America.* London: Weidenfeld and Nicolson.

[188] Stull, Donald D. 1972. "Victims of Modernization: Accident Rates and Papago Indian Ad-

justment." *Human Organization* 31:227-40.

*[189] Swanton, John Reed. 1952. *The Indian Tribes of North America*. Smithsonian Institution, Bureau of American Ethnology, Bulletin:145. Washington D.C.: U. S. Government Printing Office. (Reprinted, 1968.)

[190] Taylor, Herbert C., Jr. 1963. "Aboriginal Populations of the Lower Northwest Coast." *Pacific Northwest Quarterly* (Oct.) 54:158-65.

[191] Taylor, Herbert C., Jr. and Hoaglin, Lester L., Jr. 1962. "The 'Intermittent Fever' Epidemic of the 1830's on the Lower Columbia River." *Ethnohistory* 9:160-178.

[192] Teitelbaum, Michael S. 1975. "Relevance of Demographic Transition Theory for Developing Countries." *Science* 188:420-25.

[193] Temple, Wayne Calhoun. 1966. *Indian Villages of the Illinois Country. Historic Tribes*. Illinois State Museum Scientific Papers:2, pt. 2. Springfield, Ill.: Illinois State Museum.

[194] Termer, Franz. 1951. "The Density of Population in the Southern and Northern Maya Empires as an Archaeological and Geographical Problem." In *Selected Papers of the 29th International Congress of Americanists, 3 vols., ed. Sol Tax,* vol. 1, *The Civilizations of Ancient America,* pp. 101-107. Chicago: University of Chicago Press. (Reprinted, New York: Cooper Square, 1967.)

[195] Thiel, David H. Van; Gavaler, Judith; and Lester, Roger. 1974. "Ethanol Inhibition of Vitamin A Metabolism in the Testes: Possible Mechanism for Sterility in Alcoholics." *Science* 186:941–42.

[196] Thompson, H. Paul. 1966. "Estimating Aboriginal American Population: A Technique Using Anthropological and Biological Data." *Current Anthropology* 7:417–24.

[197] Tinker, Sylvester. n.d. *Authentic Osage Indian Roll Book.* Pawhuska, Okla.: Sam McClain.

[198] Turner, B. L., 2nd. 1974. "Prehistoric Intensive Agriculture in the Mayan Lowlands." *Science* 185:118–24.

[199] Twitchell, Edward W. 1925. "The California Pandemic of 1833." *California and Western Medicine* 23:592–93.

[200] Tyroler, Herman A. and Patrick, Ralph. 1972. "Epidemiologic Studies of Papago Indian Mortality." *Human Organization* 31:163–70.

[201] Ubelaker, Douglas H. 1974. *Reconstruction of Demographic Profiles from Ossuary Skeletal Samples: A Case Study from the Tidewater Potomac.* Smithsonian Contributions to Anthropology:

18. Washington, D.C.: Smithsonian Institution Press.

[202] Uhlmann, Julie M. 1972. "The Impact of Modernization on Papago Indiana Fertility." *Human Organization* 31:149–61.

United States, Bureau of the Census [formerly Census Office].

[203] 1894. *Report of Indians Taxed and Indians Not Taxed in the United States (excluding Alaska) at the Eleventh Census: 1890.* Washington, D.C.: Government Printing Office.

[204] 1915. *Indian Population in the United States and Alaska. 1910.* Washington, D.C.: Government Printing Office.

[205] 1937. *Fifteenth Census of the United States: 1930. The Indian Population of the United States and Alaska* ... Washington, D.C.: U. S. Government Printing Office.

[206] 1973. *Census of the Population: 1970. Subject Reports. Final Report PC (2)–1F American Indians.* Washington, D.C.: U. S. Government Printing Office.

[207] Unrau, William E. 1973. "The Depopulation of the Dheghia–Siouan Kansa Prior to Removal." *New Mexico Historical Review* 48:313–28.

[208] Whittaker, James O. 1963. "Alcohol and the Standing Rock Sioux Tribe, II: Psychodynamics and Cultural Factors in Drinking." *Quarterly Journal of Studies on Alcohol* 24:80–91.

[209] Williams, Herbert U. 1909. "The Epidemic of the Indians of New England, 1616–1620, with Remarks on Native American Infections." *John Hopkins Hospital Bulletin* 20:340–49.

Wissler, Clark.

[210] 1936. *Changes in Population Profiles Among the Northern Plains Indians.* American Museum of Natural History, Anthropological Papers:36, pt. 1. New York: American Museum of Natural History.

[211] 1936. "Distribution of Death Among American Indians." *Human Biology* 8:223–31.

[212] 1936. *Population Changes Among the Northern Plains Indians.* Yale University Publications in Anthropology:1. New Haven: For the Section of Anthropology, Department of the Social Sciences, Yale University.

[213] Wolff, Peter H. 1973. "Vasomotor Sensitivity to Alcohol in Diverse Mongoloid Populations." *American Journal of Human Genetics* 25:193–99.

[214] Wood, Corinne Shear. 1975. "New Evidence for a Late Introduction of Malaria into the New World." *Current Anthropology* 16:93–104.

[215] Woodward, William E.; Hirschorn, Norbert; Sack, R. Bradley; Cash, Richard A.; Inez, Brownlee; Chickadonz, Grace H.; Evans, Lois K.; Shepard, Richard H.; and Woodward, R. Craig. 1974. "Acute Diarrhea on an Apache Indian Reservation." *American Journal of Epidemiology* 99:281–90.

[216] Workman, Peter L. and Niswander, Jerry D. 1970. "Population Studies in Southwestern Indian Tribes. II. Local Genetic Differentiation in the Papago." *American Journal of Human Genetics* 22:24–49.

[217] Zubrow, Ezra B. W. 1974. *Population, Contact, and Climate in the New Mexican Pueblos.* Anthropological Papers of the University of Arizona:24. Tucson: University of Arizona Press.

The Newberry Library
Center for the History of the American Indian

Director: Francis Jennings

Established in 1972 by the Newberry Library, in conjunction with the Committee on Institutional Cooperation of eleven midwestern universities, the Center makes the resources of one of America's foremost research libraries in the Humanities available to those interested in improving the quality and effectiveness of teaching American Indian history. The Newberry's collections include some 100,000 volumes on the history of the American Indian and offer specialized resources for studying historical aspects of Indian–White relations and Indian linguistics. The Center also assists Native Americans engaged in writing tribal histories and developing educational materials.

ADVISORY COMMITTEE

Chairman: D'Arcy McNickle

Robert F. Berkhofer
University of Michigan

Robert V. Dumont, Jr.
*Fort Peck Tribal
Health Department*

Raymond D. Fogelson
University of Chicago

William T. Hagan
*State University of
New York College, Fredonia*

Robert F. Heizer
*University of California,
Berkeley*

Nancy O. Lurie
Milwaukee Public Museum

N. Scott Momaday
Standford University

Alfonso Ortiz
University of New Mexico

Father Peter J. Powell
*The Newberry Library and
St. Augustine Indian Center*

Father Paul Prucha, S.J.
Marquette University

Sol Tax
University of Chicago

Robert K. Thomas
*Montieth College,
Wayne State University*

Robert M. Utley
*United States National
Park Service*

Dave Warren
*Institute of American
Indian Arts*

Wilcomb E. Washburn
Smithsonian Institution